Communication and Language, and Physical Development. The specific areas will be Expressive Arts and Design, Literacy, Understanding the World, and Mathematics. The high profile of Personal, Social and Emotional Development is admirable and signifies its centrality to children's learning. It also lays responsibility on practitioners to deepen and broaden their own understanding of young children's social and emotional understanding. A key part of this process is to recognise the way in which our behaviour is impacted on by our emotions and social understanding. Children's (and adult's) behaviour is, as you will discover, a complex topic and there are many aspects which deserve considerably more attention than can be afforded in this book.

How to use this book

This book has been set out to be read from cover to cover or to be dipped into as necessary. It can fulfil several roles, for instance, as an introduction to some of the current issues related to the understanding of young children's behaviour. It is also an opportunity to develop your practice, based on the main text in each chapter, but supported with points for reflection and links with your practice to help identify specific methods of improvement. In addition, it can be a starting point for further reading, research and learning about different aspects of children's behaviour. This includes theoretical perspectives, specific influences such as emotions, social interactions and behaviour.

There are some consistent themes throughout the book. Firstly, the importance of engaging with parents and families as you develop your understanding of each individual child's behaviour. Secondly, the need to build a shared understanding between staff members of the core values and beliefs about early social, emotional and behavioural learning. Thirdly, building on this shared understanding to articulate the key messages which will be communicated through your daily practice and interactions with both children and adults. Finally, that as adults it is our role, especially in early years provision, to scaffold children's learning and work with all involved adults to give each child the 'best possible chance' to positively learn about and understand about themselves and others.

The examples of practice are the result of observations and reflections with practitioners during training sessions as well as visits to early years provision. The examples given are composites, sometimes from more than one visit or setting. They are intended to give a realistic flavour of how the main

text can be used to inform real life situations and effective practice. They have been selected because they illustrate ways in which practitioners have worked with parents to resolve some issues related to behaviour which are a regular feature of conversations with practitioners.

The books recommended are readily available through local or college libraries and various online bookstores. Journal references can be followed up via the Internet (Google will find most of them) or alternatively local or college libraries will be able to access them.

The process of learning for both children and adults requires opportunities to received new information, think about the relation to existing knowledge and communicate to others. Deep level learning needs engagement in each of these stages in order to really make changes in our thinking and understanding. Reading this book is a first step and will either affirm or challenge your current thinking and practice. The second step is to think about and try out some of the ideas, returning to the text to reflect on the responses received. Finally, sharing with other adults your experience enables the development of thoughts into articulation which facilitates the process of real learning.

Learning is a core part of making sense of experience and gaining confidence in our own competencies. As an adult learner it is useful to find out what helps your learning and enables you to build confidence and skill which will improve your practice.

Learning how the world works

Chapter 1

JS9264
372.21 MAT
SNOWSTONE

Thinking about behaviour as an area of learning

Of all areas of learning, the one that raises most concern and most celebration, especially when children are very young, is behaviour. However, very quickly adults seem to think about the word 'behaviour' as a mainly negative concept. A particular focus of this book is to think in some depth about behaviour as a normal part of children's early learning and development. Perhaps the easiest way to begin this thinking is to acknowledge 'behaviour' as everything we do and everything we say. A baby's first smile, first step, giving something to another, are all behavioural milestones which should be celebrated. A baby's cry, spitting out something which tastes unpleasant, reaching for a toy held by another, are also important behavioural responses. Fundamentally, our behaviour is a means of communication and for children who are not yet verbally confident, it is their major means of giving messages about their needs and emotions. 'Behavioural learning' is a phrase which describes the learning which takes place and helps us to understand how we can change, and use our behaviour as well as the impact it can have on situations and relationships.

Generally in society, there is concern about the behaviour of children and young people. Through television, Internet, magazines and newspapers we are made very aware of child, teenage and adult behaviours which are negative. As adults we often have an interest in such information in order to highlight how 'good' our own family members are and how well they behave. However, such information can also raise anxiety, particularly for parents of young children as they set out to prevent their children developing such negative behaviours. In each of our early years settings there are likely to be individuals and groups of children whose behaviour already causes us concern. For a variety of reasons they may respond to others in ways that you do not consider to be appropriate.

Although the home learning environment has been shown to have most impact (Sylva, Melhuish, Sammons, Siraj-Blatchford, & Taggart, 2010), some of our young children spend up to fifty hours per week in childcare provision, so the influence we

as early educators can have on young children's behavioural learning is significant. If we can work positively with parents to support the child's developing understanding about behaviour, this influence is increased considerably. The more we can engage with parents, the more effective our support for children's learning.

We hear a lot about early intervention being effective in preventing future difficulties in all areas of learning, (Cabinet Office 2009, 2010), particularly in the context of behaviour. However, it is not always easy to work out what that 'early intervention' might look like on a daily basis in our own setting. In order to think about this constructively, it is important to reflect on what we know about how children learn to behave.

We all experience behaviour every minute of every day, we cannot avoid being influenced by the interactions we come across. Young children especially are looking to those bigger than them, both adults and children, to learn how the world works and what is important for them to know. The experiences children have help to build a picture for them of how people relate to each other. As children get older, patterns of behaviour emerge and become characteristic ways of responding. Early intervention is about providing opportunities for children to experience and learn from positive relationships and supportive adults to help them gain understanding which will enable them to establish and maintain their own positive social connections.

Early Intervention

Early intervention is not just about at an early stage in life, but also at the point that early signs are noted that may indicate emerging difficulties. We can all understand that prevention is better than a cure, and this is particularly true when supporting behavioural learning. If we invest in and create an environment that enables positive learning about behaviour, we can show children effective and appropriate ways of interacting.

Understanding Behaviour in the Early Years

A practical guide to supporting each child's behaviour in the early years setting

Kay Mathieson

Contents

Early years and behavioural learning	2
Thinking about behaviour as an area of learning	4
Engaging with parents	6
Building parents' confidence, building practitioners' understanding	9
Creating a context for parents to help each other	10
Research and theories about behaviour	15
Attachment	16
Approaches to behaviour	17
Cultural considerations	18
Developing a setting approach to behaviour	20
Brain development	20
Conditions for growth	27
Thinking about social learning	32
Social competence	33
Friendships	34
Conflicts	37
Thinking about emotional learning	39
Communicating emotions	39
Regulating emotions	43
Thinking about behavioural learning	44
Policy and practice	44
Influences on behaviour	45
Temperament	46
Using observation and analysis	50
Interpreting observations	51
Identifying the learning	52
Pretend play	53
Using 'can do' statements	54
Special Educational Needs	58
References	61
Additional sources of information	62
Finding help and support	63
Acknowledgments	64

Published by Practical Pre-School Books, A Division of MA Education Ltd, St Jude's Church, Dulwich Road, Herne Hill, London, SE24 0PB.

Tel: 020 7738 5454

www.practicalpreschoolbooks.com

© MA Education Ltd 2012

All images © MA Education Ltd., other than the images listed below:

Front cover images: Top left: © iStockphoto.com/Vanessa Morosini, Bottom left: © iStockphoto.com/Liza McCorkle

All photos other than the above taken by Ben Suri and Lucie Carlier.

ISBN 978-1-907241-22-2

Early Childhood Essentials

059264

Early years and behavioural learning

Being sociable with others

Having fun together

The purpose of this book is to offer both a starting point and a step to further learning about children's early social, emotional and behavioural learning. Working with young children can be fascinating and intriguing, but it is also challenging and frustrating. Children do not set out to upset the adults or children around them, but they are trying to make sense of how relationships and interactions work. When we are with children we are role models showing them how things work. It is important to remember that children will not select only the aspects of our behaviour we want them to imitate!

In this book the term 'setting' is used to describe any early years provision and includes, childminders, pre-schools, day nurseries, reception classes, nursery schools, nursery classes, etc. 'Practitioner' is used as an inclusive description of the professionals who work in early years, regardless of their current level of qualification. The word 'parent' is employed to signify the child's main carers. However, it is recognised that there are many important people for children in their families. It is for practitioners in their knowledge of the individual child to understand the valuable relationships which exist and nurture the child's development. Ultimately, as professionals it is for the practitioners to be proactive in establishing and maintaining a positive partnership with all parents. In their role as advocates for each child, practitioners will seek out ways to build parents' confidence in supporting their child's developmental progress.

At the time of writing, the Early Years Foundation Stage has been reviewed by Dame Clare Tickell and the consultation of the government response is currently taking place. It seems likely that, as recommended through the review that there will be three prime, and four specific areas of learning. The prime areas will be Personal, Social and Emotional Development,

However, this is often easier said than done as it involves all practitioners demonstrating what this looks like in their interactions with children, parents and colleagues consistently every day. In addition, this positive approach needs to be applied to more difficult situations, like sorting out conflicts and the inevitable squabbles which are all part of learning how to get on with each other. When children and adults experience sensitive and empathetic engagement to resolve conflicts, they receive important messages about understanding others' feelings and vocalising emotions appropriately. If this is done well it is likely to reduce the need for children to escalate to more challenging behaviours in order to communicate their needs (Meadows, 2010 p175, Rubin, Bukowski & Parker, 2006). It will also help children to understand that, when we do not agree or if we want the same thing at the same time, there are many ways to resolve the situation. In essence we will be helping children to see situations from different perspectives and recognise the emotions which may be involved.

A crucial part of learning about our behaviour and the way in which we interact with others is to recognise our own perspective and to develop our understanding of how others may see the situation. This is a very complex process and it develops gradually as children experience different relationships and learn about how the world works. Such understanding of others' thinking is not really fully developed until children are about five years old (Wellman, Cross, & Watson, 2001).

The child's view

In early years provision, our first approach to making a positive impact on children's behaviour is to try to see the experience of coming to our setting through the eyes of each individual child. For some children this will be a happy and exciting experience, for others it will be filled with anxiety and fear, but for most it will be a mixture of the full range of emotions, sometimes on a daily basis. As practitioners, we need to be learning about the ways in which each child expresses these emotions. The best source of knowledge is a combination of listening to parents' observations of their child and sharing with other educators our own observations. Parents begin learning about their child from the moment they are born, and by the time the child comes to attend an early years setting they have an extensive amount of understanding and knowledge about their child. However, on meeting professional childcare practitioners, parents can often undervalue the extent and importance of their own specialist knowledge. It is key to establishing a positive relationship that practitioners enable parents to recognise that their insights are valued and help to inform the approaches and strategies which are used to support their child's learning in the setting. Recent research suggests that there may currently be patterns of communication between parents and practitioners which change over time. For example, when children are younger, about two years old, parents and practitioners have been

Doing things together

Learning from adults

found to agree in their views of positive behaviours, but not negative behaviours. But at three to four years, agreement between parents and practitioners was related more to negative behaviours (Mathieson & Banerjee, 2010). One possible explanation is that as children are more able to have positive interactions, adults talk more about the exception of the difficult behaviours which occur. Alternatively, it could be that the focus in the setting is more about noticing and commenting on negative behaviours. Through reflecting on our current practice in communicating with parents, we can be sure to maintain a balance between talking about positive and less positive behaviours.

Engaging with parents

Through practitioners' earliest observations of children's interactions and by listening to parents, they are able to develop an awareness of how children may be feeling at different times. Understanding the emotions, as well as talking with parents and colleagues about possible ways to respond, really helps to give children consistent and supportive messages about their behaviour. This is true of encouraging positive behaviour as well as helping to change specific negative behaviours.

Considering that behaviour and interactions are so complex, it is amazing that the majority of children will, for most of the time, behave in ways which we consider to be appropriate for their age and experience. This mainly positive experience also allows the adults a sense of being in control of the situation. However, as soon as a child demonstrates behaviour which for us, as individuals, feels beyond our expectation, we can easily feel overwhelmed, deskilled, frustrated and at a loss as to the best way to respond. Systems of support between adults are a significant positive influence on the emotional environment in which children learn about relationships and caring for each other. Problem solving about what might be leading to a particular behavioural response or which might be the best way to react should not be left to any one individual, but is much more effective if done together with all the adults who care for the child. Initially, this would be members of the room team and parents but may be extended to include the SENCO, Leaders or managers (see Chapter 6 for suggestions about collating information and engaging with other support agencies).

As adults we can often struggle to make sense of our role, both as parents and professionals, in relation to children. This is particularly true when thinking about behaviour and

making problematic decisions about which levels of control are appropriate at different times. Today there are many sources of information about children's health and development with a vast array of advice and guidance. This is available at the touch of a button via the Internet, but also from friends, family and sometimes complete strangers! The result is that this can be a confusing muddle of contradictory messages, very few of which actually take into account the characteristics and circumstances of the individual child. By working together and by building a shared understanding of the unique child and their needs, parents and practitioners can benefit from each other's knowledge of the child as they learn to respond to the very different social demands of home and setting life.

It is essential to engage with parents from the first contact to make them feel welcome and set the scene for constructive relationship to develop. A regular review of routines for answering the phone, showing parents round on visits, as well as daily arrivals and departures is a useful way to continually improve relationships with parents. Finding a variety of ways to ask parents and family members for feedback about how it feels to come to your setting is also really important in improving your practice.

Principles and values

For general interactions to be consistently positive with all parents, staff will need to understand and recognise how to communicate the principles and values of the setting in all their interactions with parents. Underpinning this is the belief that engaging and supporting positive communication with parents is crucial for the children's well-being. It is all too easy to start off this process positively, but as soon as there is a difficult interaction, consider the parent as not interested or unhelpful. As professionals, it is our role to make an effort and to maintain and build relationships with all parents. As Marion Dowling points out, all families are different, but helping them to feel confident in their parenting is of great benefit to young children (Dowling, 2005). The start of this process could be making practical decisions about how the communication will take place. Some parents' preference will be for the full range of forms of communication: email, text, letter, face-to-face, photographs, and slide presentations. A major part of communication with parents is about working out which is the best method for particular purposes. Establishing different ways of communicating with parents includes negotiating times, method and purpose of daily, weekly, monthly or yearly contact. It also involves considering how the method of communication is influenced by the purpose, for example, celebrations, talking about difficulties, one-off or ongoing issues. Communication is, of course, a two-way process and it is important to make sure that it is effective, whether initiated by parents or practitioners.

Knowing your parents is crucial to maintaining good relationships and as an investment for when you need to work positively through any difficult times. Building on your local knowledge of the area through talking to individual parents and families, can help you to understand why certain situations are more challenging for some families than for others. Through this understanding it is much easier to complement the home-based relationships and provide more appropriate support for the child.

First conversations

The beginning of this process is based on information, collected through your usual admission procedure. Rather than just collecting basic information this is an opportunity to communicate how much you value the knowledge parents already have about their children. It is most effective if this is part of a conversation rather than a structured question and answer or form-filling activity. Open-ended questions which are focused on an understanding of the child's current experience can be helpful to begin a shared awareness understanding of how the child might react to attendance at the setting.

Being together

POINT FOR REFLECTION

What is working well in your contact and communication with parents and extended families?

Think about the systems of contact and communication which you have with parents. Which do you think are most effective? In reviewing each one you may want to consider the following:

- Do parents think the same systems are effective as you do?

- Do you have regular, frequent and positive contact with all parents?

- For the parents you have least contact with, which way of communicating works best for them?

- For the parents you have most contact with, what is it that makes it easier for both parties to maintain the links?

- Do you actively seek the views of parents whose children have moved on from your provision?

- Do you actively seek the views of parents who visited but did not take up a place at your provision?

From a parent's perspective, deciding to bring their child to you can be a difficult and anxious time for all sorts of reasons. They will feel a wide range of emotions including some of the following:

- You, as the professional, will criticise their parenting or their child

- They don't know enough about childcare settings to be confident that they have chosen the right one

- Generally anxious about leaving their child

- They have had a poor experience at a previous setting which they do not want to tell you about

- You will not understand their child's communication about their needs

- You will not be an advocate for their child

The things which might be helpful to talk about before Alesha begins attending could include:

1. A typical week for Alesha.
2. Her favourite places, why might she like them?
3. Which of her extended family are particularly important to her? Given a choice, who does she like to be with?
4. What opportunities has she had to play with younger or older children in ones, twos or larger groups? Is she more at ease with smaller or larger groups of children her age?

5. What sort of indoor activities does she like?
6. What sort of outdoor activities does she like?
7. Which local parks, libraries, swimming pools is she familiar with?

From these sorts of questions you can begin to build a picture of the situations and activities which are familiar to Alesha. This will help you to think with parents about which of the setting experiences are going to be most like or different from her previous experiences. More importantly it especially helps to be able to talk to her about things that she has experienced and important people so that she understands you are interested and value her important people too. There is no need for these to be questions on a form to fill in, or completed in one session; better for them to be a part of a conversation which can then be added to or amended over time as you get to know the family better.

To increase your understanding and insight about what it feels like for a parent coming to your setting, it can be useful to ask for their reflections of those first few weeks when their child attended. There are a variety of ways which this can be done and it is important to remember that it is the more detailed or less positive comments which often help to improve practice the most. For example, if a parent tells us everything was wonderful it is hard to understand which of the things we did were most supportive. We can also be left with a vague idea that we have got everything right and cannot improve, which is very unlikely to be the case. Each group of parents (and practitioners) is different and the ways in which

LINKS WITH YOUR PRACTICE

Although behaviour is an area we get most concerned about, it is also often the topic we find it most difficult to talk about. This may be because we tend not to talk about it until there is a problem or because we are not sure what we need to be discussing. Sometimes our everyday conversations with parents can be reduced to a list of food, nappy changes/ toileting and if the child has had a good, bad or indifferent day overall. In some ways this is a safe, easy list, which both parents and practitioners can feel comfortable with and becomes a regular routine which rapidly loses significance. Whilst it is important that parents are well-informed about such things, what is significant is when there is a change or unexpected difference in a child's eating or toileting. For example, a child who normally eats every meal with enthusiasm is suddenly reluctant to eat or only eats a small amount. Further discussion and ideas about working in partnership with parents and effective communication methods can be found in a range of books such as Jennie Lindon's *Parents as Partners* (Lindon, 2009).

Using daily conversations to build up a picture of children's individual social connections and experiences with parents can really help to reduce parents anxieties and consolidate their trust in you. Through sharing developments in engaging with others, pretend play skills, social language and resolving conflicts, parents become involved in understanding how complex this can be for children. They are also helped to recognise realistic expectations of children at particular ages and stages. Finally, opening up the conversation provides an opportunity for sharing concerns about social interactions which may occur at home. This shared problem solving can be very supportive of children's learning in the early stages of developing positive social connections.

Appreciating each other's skills

they interact change as they get to know each other more. If we can make inviting feedback from parents a frequent and regular part of our practice, we are more likely to consolidate respectful professional relationships. This gives parents the message that we are willing to listen, consider and work together to improve practice.

Parents' views

Possible ways to gather parents' views include:

- Individual conversations with practitioners

- Interactive display boards, such as an outline of how things are now – "When new parents come for their first visit we".... "We would like to make this a welcoming and positive experience, in what ways could we make it better?" Post-it notes are then available for parents and practitioners to add a quick comment or suggestion. This is best developed through practitioners also talking to parents about the display board when they pick up a drop off children. If suggestions are offered in the conversation practitioners can add them to the board

- Comments box with blank postcards available to write on – most useful if there is a specific question or focus to prompt everyone's thinking. For example, "We are planning an event for parents to meet each other and hear about

what goes on at nursery What would you like to be included in the event?" Some further prompts like, food, information, activities, length of time, day of the week with question marks can also increase parent response. Do consider setting realistic expectations. For example, if you cannot be flexible about the day of the week, be sure not to ask for suggestions of which day suits parents

- Voting boxes (ideally see-through) – one question such as: "Would you prefer to meet with staff to discuss your child's progress between 8:30 – 9:30 or 4:30 – 6:30?" Tokens are then posted to register the parent's preference. If the boxes are see through parents are also able to see the majority vote which is likely then to inform your final decision

- Inviting a couple of parents to talk to and gather others' views about a particular issue

- Giving one or two practitioners time to contact parents to gather views about a specific issue

- Establishing a parents' group or forum can help to ensure parental views are being taken into account in your plans for improvement

You will no doubt use a variety of methods to gather parents' views and it is always worth asking parents how they would like their views collected. Many working parents will have experience of market research or customer relations and be able to contribute suggestions of tried and tested ways to gather feedback.

Building parents' confidence, building practitioners' understanding

Being a parent is a very complex job and, like practitioners, they are likely to feel more confident at some stages of the child's development than others. A baby can be seen as predictable, totally dependent and manageable once routines have been established. Alternatively, they can be seen as the scariest, most fragile treasure for which you have total responsibility. Similarly, toddlers, preschool, and school-aged children can be lively, interesting and exciting to be with or frustrating, challenging and exhausting. Practitioners often have some degree of choice over the age range they work with, but parents have to develop confidence and skill to

Relaxed and happy - ready to learn

contend with all stages. Parents may begin with very clear ideas about what their parenting experience will be like and their approaches to the inevitable challenges of supporting their children's learning and development. However, many influences, such as changes in circumstances, sleep deprivation, unsettled crying babies and the range of advice and suggestions which bombard new parents, can quickly lead to feelings of being overwhelmed and confused. These feelings may be temporary or longer lasting.

Talking with parents about observations of their child and encouraging them to contribute their own observations is a very effective way to develop a shared understanding of both the child's behaviour and the parent's confidence at the current stage of development. There are various ways to begin this discussion including:

- Using a photograph of the child engaged in an activity and talking through the context, learning, interactions and responses of the child

- Reflecting on a series of observation notes related to a child's particular interest to highlight progress over a short time

- Building on a parent's description of a family outing or event and using sensitive questioning to highlight skills the child is developing

Creating a context for parents to help each other

Most parents are very busy and would find committing a lot of time to setting activities regularly very difficult. However, some will be willing and happy to support other parents as an occasional or one-off event. For example, when parents first begin to attend the setting, contact with another parent to talk through concerns or organisational problems might be useful. Using display boards and noticeboards with prompts such as photographs, learning journeys and questions about the local area are easy ways to start parents talking to each other. It is also helpful for parents to share knowledge about local facilities and amenities.

For example:

- A map of the local area showing parks and playgrounds can easily be downloaded from the Internet (often on local council websites or through Internet-based searches). Parents are then able to add post-it notes about their visits, offering useful information about buses, cafes, toilets and ranges of equipment for younger or older children etc. An outing led by the practitioners might also encourage a parent new to the area or anxious about going alone to come along. Sometimes parents will also begin to arrange trips together to share the responsibility and enable children to play together with friends

Positive early relationships really matter

Family and friends teach us about relationships

Example: Tuning into individuals

Do we value all learning?

Childminder

Marina was working with a young mum whose toddler (Aaron) was very interested in keys. He had begun to pick up keys wherever he saw them, hiding them, holding them and sometimes giving them to Mum. Marina had also noticed his interest in keys. Through discussion Mum and Marina realised what an important feature of daily life keys must seem to Aaron. Adults were often looking for, holding, picking up, handing to each other or using keys. Marina listened in detail as Mum talked about the family routines about keys. It seemed possible that Aaron could be included more in the routines, by using the phrase "Where should we put the keys?" when they came into the house each time and letting Aaron put the keys in the drawer. This was amended to "Where do we keep the keys?" and when it was time to get them out of the drawer and Aaron was able to take them out of the drawer and give them to either Mum or Dad. Aaron was now being praised and cuddled for finding them, this helped to include him in what was going on and give a positive purpose to the interest in keys. Mum felt that it was more effective than saying "no" every time he went near the keys and highlighted Aaron's delight in being helpful and receiving praise.

Day nursery

The Happy Days Day Nursery was alerted to the anxieties children were feeling about moving rooms during a parent Tea and Talk session. The parents also told the practitioners that they found it confusing and that getting used to new staff took a little while. As a first step the staff developed a new routine with the help of the parents. When children were about to move into a new room there was a special hand-over meeting with parents and both the key persons. This was an opportunity to talk about all of the child's learning but especially the important behavioural learning which had been achieved. Parents and practitioners were able to think together about each child's emotional well-being and what might trigger anxieties. A discussion which, although unplanned, became a core part of the conversation was recognising early signals that the child was feeling anxious. The 'new key person' also set out the general developmental changes in behaviour which were likely to occur during the coming year. The adults shared experiences of things which parents in the past have worried about and ways in which these issues have been resolved. They organised arrangements for regular sharing

Example: Tuning into individuals

Interacting is a fundamental aspect of learning

of ideas and progress. A key topic was finding the easiest way to communicate or indicate the need for a discussion. This included email, text, phone call and a prearranged signal at the beginning or end of the day.

Pre-school

At Jolly Roger's Pre-school they started a September meeting of 'old' and 'new' parents with coffee and snacks. They talked specifically about ways of helping children to join in others' play and different ways to resolve conflicts. The parents were encouraged to talk with each other about local parks they had visited and the activities their children enjoyed. This informal discussion led to several families meeting up at their local park and trying out some of the ways suggested to help their children join in games.

Discussions developed about, how children were approaching others to engage in play, which activities they most like to share with other children and how parents recognise if their child is anxious, sad or worried. Many positive messages about behaviour were shared which established a positive relationship. It also gave

clear messages about practitioner's interest in the child's development and understanding about the pressures of parenting.

School

Wheatfield Primary School invited a small group of parents from Year 1 children with the parent-governor to meet the new reception class parents. The first of these sessions was so successful in identifying and exploring parent and children's anxieties that the parents asked if it could be repeated. The parent-governor organised meetings on a termly basis for snacks, drinks and chat sessions. A variety of different days and times of day were used, such as the end of school day, early morning, Saturday etc to accommodate as many parents as possible. Each meeting also voted for a focus topic ready for the next meeting e.g., mealtimes, bedtimes, Internet safety, behaviour and resolving conflicts. There were no guest speakers arranged but everyone tried to find out what they could to bring to the next meeting to support each other. The school leadership team used some of the suggestions as topics for parents' evenings with a guest speaker invited.

- No one setting can provide all the support a parent and family might need, so it is really important to explore and be aware of local sources of support for families. A good starting point is to develop a relationship with your nearest Children's Centres and share with parents the activities and support which they can access

- Check out and establish a contact with local libraries, GP surgeries, health visitors, local settings involved in the Every Child a Talker programme, and speech and language therapy groups (ECaT/Salt), dieticians, midwives, special educational needs (SEN) support teams, families information service, children's centres, local schools, local park activities, family friendly activities and spaces. Remember, not all families need all the available information all of the time, so it is important that parents are clear about how to access support from practitioners, and for practitioners to be sensitive in signposting services and support

The local area around your setting is usually the area of most interest to the parents who bring their children to you, so developing your knowledge about what is available can be very useful. If your parents tend to choose your setting because it is close to their work their view of the area may be different, so it may be useful to add to local information with a map showing where parents commute from so that there are opportunities for families to make links if they wish.

Positively engaging parents and families

It can be helpful to think about what might be the 'magnets' to attract your parents and families to events and encourage closer involvement with your setting. The obvious one is, of course, their children, but others such as food, refreshments, new experiences and shared activities can come a close second.

Early years settings, particularly in cities, often find that there are many nationalities and ethnicities represented in the parents and families who attend their provision. A successful way of encouraging engagement in the setting community is to offer a range of food for all to try and share. Ideally, some parents will be involved in the planning and the sourcing of the food. In most cultures food and eating serve a social purpose and can be a good opportunity for developing conversations. Practitioners' attitudes will play

a key role in building the confidence of parents and positively supporting interactions between parents to make the event a success. It is also a useful opportunity to talk with parents and families about mealtime expectations of children, and to respectfully compare similarities and differences between home and setting.

All adults feel confident and are good at something and most, with a little encouragement, are willing to share this with others. For example, a practitioner in a children's centre discovered that a Mum had good dressmaking skills. Through discussion the Mum agreed to make some clothes for the children to use in their role play. Rather than the parent doing this at home, the Mum was invited to come to the centre so that the children were aware of the work being done. As a result the children were engaged in discussion with the Mum about sewing, making things and shared experiences of members of their family who made things too. This also provided an opportunity for children to just to sit and engage in conversation while the Mum was sewing, a real treasure for young children when adults often seem so busy.

Extended family connections vary and are less close when relatives move to other areas to find work. As a result, new parents can become isolated and lack advice from trusted experienced family members about childcare and parenting. Opportunities through early years settings to talk about worries and celebrations can really help to build confidence for both Mums and Dads. Parents are inevitably trying to do their best for their children and to make their lives better than the parent's own experience. Sharing with parents, your knowledge and understanding of child development and looking together for exciting milestones such as rolling over, beginning to crawl, first steps etc creates a joint interest and basis for in-depth discussion about the child's progress. A particularly helpful approach is to consider with parents the sorts of learning and experiences which are significant for children at specific ages. What is it like to be two, six, ten months or two, three, four or five years old? Sharing our knowledge about child development helps to give a context for children's responses and behaviours. This can increase the likelihood of adults seeing the world from the child's perspective and responding in a way which supports the child's learning. Further information can be found in a range of resources including the *What does it mean to be...?* series (Lindon, 2008/9).

A practical way to support these discussions could be through photograph and comment booklets for each age range in the setting compiled by parents and practitioners. Experienced

Understanding you understanding me

- Feeding
- Toileting

- Is my child normal, do all children respond like this?
  - Repeating actions over and over again
  - Hitting out to make contact with others
  - Putting everything in their mouths
  - Crying when parents leave them

- Why would children behave in this way?
  - Copying actions they have watched others doing
  - Refusing help to put on shoes then getting frustrated when they can't complete the task
  - Throwing or dropping things from buggies or highchairs

There are many examples, and discussions with parents will provide many more. Searching together for an answer through observation, reading or asking others can be as supportive as being able to offer an immediate explanation.

Using the approach of considering the described behaviour in its' developmental context is an important first step. For example, making contact with others by hitting or touching is very common when children's language is at an early stage of development. The child wants to play or engage with someone it is much quicker and more effective to make contact through touch rather than finding the right words and articulating them. Thinking with parents about words or gestures which will not be interpreted as hitting helps to support children through this phase. Working in partnership with parents helps to ensure that the suggestions build on shared knowledge of the child.

practitioners have a clear idea of the range of behaviours and progress children are likely to make while with them during baby, toddler, pre-school or reception stages. Talking with parents about these expectations, in general terms, can help to reduce anxiety and build confidence for parents. Some important things to bear in mind which often worry parents are:

- Is my child late or early at developing this skill or awareness?
  - Crawling
  - Walking
  - Talking

KEY POINTS IN THINKING ABOUT BEHAVIOUR AS AN AREA OF LEARNING

- Building positive relationships with parents and family members is important to the children's well-being and an investment for practitioners to increase the likelihood of continued positive support from parents. It increases the shared responsibility and problem solving as well as providing opportunities for celebration

- Parents and practitioners have unique contributions to make to a shared understanding of the child and their developmental progress

- First contact between parents and the staff at the setting, whether school, day nursery, pre-school, childminder or after school club will set the tone for future relationships

- Sharing progress is particularly important in understanding the development of positive social connections and behaviour patterns

- Creating a relaxed, happy but purposeful environment helps behaviour and all learning

Chapter 2

Research and theories about behaviour

Experiencing positive interactions

Finding ways to make connections

Our understanding of behaviour is influenced by our own experiences, of which society, local and family cultural norms play a major part. Understanding why individuals behave the way they do has fascinated researchers for several decades. Their findings, whether from a psychological, biological, neuro-scientific, sociological, geographical or philosophical viewpoint, gradually seep into our everyday 'folk psychology' or understanding of others and ourselves. However, it is useful to step aside and consider the traditions and research which influence us, particularly if we are involved in early years provision for our youngest children.

Beliefs and understanding about childhood and what children are have ranged from the idea of original sin and the need to beat the devil out of children, to seeing a child as a blank canvas on which carers can inscribe whatever they see fit. The parenting carers have received and their own individual experiences will influence their views. As we grow and develop as individuals we learn about different ways to interact, how our emotions change our responses and the fact that others think differently from us. Young children are mainly in the company of others as they develop understanding of interactions and accepted patterns of behaviour (Gauvin 2001, Perez & Gauvin 2007, Rogoff 2003). So the ways in which older children and adults react to each other as well as to the individual children will influence this developing understanding.

Society, as viewed by the child's carers, underpins what they consider to be the important skills, abilities, knowledge and understanding which children will need to be able to take their place as adults in the community. However, realistically we do have to recognise that it is very difficult to predict how the demands of society may change over the lifetime of the children we are working with at the moment. One of the current

Which theories about behaviour are most familiar to you?

- Which theorists have you heard of and what are the main messages of their work?
- When were the theories developed, 18th, 19th, 20th or 21st century?
- In what ways are they still applicable to your work today?
- What changes have there been in society which might mean that things should be viewed differently?

In what ways do your interactions with children reflect particular theoretical perspectives on behavioural learning?

- We often do not think consciously about what lies behind our interactions with children. However, spending regular time reflecting on what we are trying to achieve in our interactions with children can help to recognise why some approaches are more effective than others. Using phrases which scaffold children's learning rather than demand a preconceived "right answer" will dramatically change the quality of the interactions you have with children. It will also change the level of thinking which both you and the child will have to do

Which of your own views about behaviour do you recognise as developing from your culture and which from your training or later study?

- This is not something people often think about and can be quite difficult to work out. Thinking about how you learned about appropriate ways to behave with your family may give some insight into where some of your views about behaviour have developed. You may have developed approaches which mirror or directly contrast with your own experiences
- Training and studying as an adult often challenges our thinking in different ways to our learning at school. Often implementing new thinking from training or study feels difficult at first because it is unfamiliar. Recognising that working with a child's understanding about conflict is more effective in the long run will not initially overcome your feelings of frustration that the child has hurt someone again. This is where your professional role becomes particularly important and your need to prioritise the children's learning above your own immediate feelings

difficulties for parents and carers in this process is that the society in which they are bringing up their own children is vastly different and has changed very quickly from their own experience of growing up.

Particular periods of history show how the influence of current demands in society affects childhood, parenting and education. For example, parenting in the immediate post-war years in the UK could be characterised as ensuring children were able to conform to social rules in order to do well at school, go on to get a job, which tended to be one job for an individual's whole working life, to earn money and to be able to support their own family. The experiences of war, including rationing, military service and lack of material possessions, no doubt had a strong influence on the priorities parents had for their children. More recently, the ready availability of material goods, employment mobility (it is now more likely that individuals will have several different jobs in different geographical areas), high unemployment, instant communication such as mobile phones, electronic social networking, access to an extensive range of information via the Internet albeit of varying quality, will also impact directly on carers' priorities for children's learning.

Both parenting approaches and education systems take time to adjust to such significant changes in society. Any adjustments are also not uniform. With different families, schools and settings respond in a range of ways depending on the experiences of the individuals who are engaged in the organisation. For example, some early years settings use social networking sites and text messaging to contact parents, while others view this as inappropriate and prefer newsletters, phone calls and face to face discussion. In most cases staff groups make decisions about using different forms of communication for different purposes and think through which information is best communicated through which media.

Attachment

The researchers who have explored children's development, behaviour and learning are also a product of the families, societies and cultures in which they lived. It is useful to recognise this as a key influence on their perspectives. For example, Richard Bowlby describes how in his view the fact that his father John was distressed by having to adjust to a new family nanny may have led to his lifelong interest in early attachment (Bowlby 2010).

Bowlby's work individually and with Mary Ainsworth focused on the very early relationships established between babies and their immediate carers (Ainsworth et al., 1978, Bowlby 1969, 1973, 1980). This research has stood the test of time and is still seen as an important factor in understanding children's social learning. Notably, attachment is not seen as just about the one relationship with the main carer as was initially reported but the development of warm, sensitive and reciprocal relationships with all key carers. This work has strongly influenced the requirement to have established the role of Key Person in early years provision in the UK. The importance of the quality of attachment in early relationships, Bowlby suggests, will establish expectations of future relationships and understanding of self. These expectations of relationships and interactions with others are likely to endure for a considerable time, but are also influenced through the development of independence and reflective thinking about experiences.

Approaches to behaviour

The main approaches to behaviour that are currently influential in thinking about young children's development fall into two broad categories, namely behaviourist and social constructivist or sociocultural.

Behaviorism has a long history and is based on the idea that behaviour is a response to specific stimuli. This approach was influential for most of the 20th century and was based on experiments which established that behavioural responses of animals and humans could be directly modified. For example, associating a frightening noise with a toy rabbit presented to a young child at the same time was shown by Watson to lead to the child being frightened of the rabbit even once the noise was no longer used (Schaffer, 1996). Other theorists who were notable behaviourists included B.F. Skinner and Ivan Pavlov. Most of the behaviourist research was carried out under laboratory conditions with both animals and humans. An implication of this approach is that, given the "correct" stimulus, all individuals will respond in the same way. This stimulus-response learning continues to influence some training such as fire drill practices but also underpins thinking about rewards for appropriate behaviour and sanctions for inappropriate behaviour. However, generally it is seen to be only part of the picture in influencing behaviour, particularly as it took no account of differences between individuals' reactions or the real life social context in which responses would normally take place. For example, rewards given in the context of nurturing, warm, supportive relationships are valued by both giver and receiver as an extension of the shared understanding of the relationship.

Lev Vygotsky, whose work has a strong influence on current thinking about young children's learning and development, takes an approach which is described as social constructivist or

Understanding intentions and motivations

Experiencing a range of emotions

LINKS WITH YOUR PRACTICE

- Talking with colleagues is an important part of developing our own thinking and reflecting on the effectiveness of our practice. Sometime discussions about behaviour arise as complaints about a particular child or a moan about how difficult one group seems to be in comparison with another. In order for discussions to be supportive of adult and child learning there needs to be a balance between reflecting on appropriate and inappropriate behaviour. A brief slot at the beginning of a staff or planning meeting can be useful. This can include problem solving as well as adding to knowledge and understanding of individual children. A format which limits the time and range of the discussion can be helpful. For example, two minutes talk about the current issue, each team member offers an observation which adds to the evidence of times when the issue does not occur. Two minutes exploring solutions which build on the exceptions suggested. Team decision made about sharing information with parents and trying out one of the strategies suggested consistently for the next three weeks

- Learning is a life-long process. We continue learning about our own and others' behaviour throughout our lives. In a work context it is important and often enlightening to seek out more information about the development of children's social understanding. This can be from a variety of sources including conversation with other staff members, college library, local library, Internet (be thoughtful about the source of Internet information – not all sources are reliable), training courses and local authority support teams

- Sharing both general and specific discussions about behaviour and social learning with parents is crucial to supporting children's learning. The more these discussions take place when there is not a specific problem, the better. Being able to talk with parents about their own observations of their children and the progress they are making helps you to understand each other and get used to talking without anxiety about behaviour

- Even with the best of intentions, it is not possible to know what someone else is really thinking. It is useful in discussions to consider at least two possible interpretations of the same situation (one of which will be positive)

sociocultural. Essentially, this approach is based on the premise that learning is a social activity and that children find out about how the world works from others around them through play, observation and experiencing interactions (Vygotsky 1978). Although generally viewed as a very positive approach, it is important to understand that learning from others can be indiscriminate so need adults to mediate for the child and help them begin to tease out understanding of others thinking and actions. This adult, or more experienced, learner role is described by Vygotsky as 'scaffolding' and is crucial to supporting learning particularly in a play context (Pound 2009, Schaffer, 1996). In terms of learning about behaviour the adult role in opening out others' thinking helps children to make sense of motivations, intentions and interpretation of actions. Crucially, this enables the development of understanding, not just of other's responses but also of the child's own. This process is gradual and involves thinking about emotions and their impact on our behaviour as well as discovering ways to regulate our own responses to others behaviour.

As the description 'social construction' implies, this approach is strongly influenced by the social context in which it occurs. Current social norms, such as children being seen and not heard or children being encouraged to explore and question, would be communicated through the process described by Vygotsky (Meadows 2010). This type of apprenticeship model has continued to be explored particularly by Barbara Rogoff (Rogoff 2003), Jeremy Carpendale and Charlie Lewis (Carpendale & Lewis 2006).

Cultural considerations

Most of the current influential theories in the UK have been developed in Europe or at least have a Western orientation. It is important in our multi-ethnic population to be aware of other influences that will be as much of an influence in a range of cultures.

At the heart of cultural differences in thinking about children are social norms in child rearing and socioeconomic pressures. Child rearing can be seen as the sole responsibility of the mother, both parents, extended family, collective groups of mothers, or the whole community. Child rearing practice develops as adult roles are defined, usually by the need to provide food and shelter for the family or community. The demands on individual parents and the support available from the community vary considerably. Currently in the UK there is heavy emphasis on individuals and their responsibility to provide for themselves and their dependents.

Example: Really engaging with parents

Fun for parents too!

Day nursery

A local day nursery organised a session for new parents to talk with their key person about the kind of adults they would like their child to be. The key person talked with parents about ways in which they could work together to show the child what this would be like. Particular themes from the discussion such as being kind, having friends and being happy emerged. These themes were displayed alongside aspects of day nursery activities which helped the children develop the understanding and learning to realise their parents' aspirations. The display was regularly added to by both staff and parents, increasingly building parents' confidence in the value of the time they spent with their children and the activities they took part in.

Childminder

An experienced childminder was concerned that one of the mums whose child she looked after was new to the area and finding it difficult to make local friends and connections. She suggested an outing to the local park at the end of the day with the three children and two mums she was currently working with. While the childminder engaged with the children the mums were encouraged to tell each other about their own growing up and how they were taught about appropriate and inappropriate behaviour. While they walked back to the childminder's house they were asked about what they wanted to be the same or different for their children. The childminder used these conversations as the basis for talking together with the mums (and later the dads) about ways to resolve conflicts between the children and develop their understanding of each other.

Pre-school

The staff of a packaway pre-school were concerned about difficulties the current group of children were having with sharing toys and equipment. At a team meeting they thought of as many different ways to respond as possible. Their solutions explored phrases to use, immediate and long term actions as well as ways to share concerns with parents. Finally, the discussion focused on why they would use different approaches with different children and parents. The staff reported that the discussions helped them feel more confident about their own responses to situations and to feel supported by their colleagues whom they now knew would respond in a similar way.

However, there is tension between this and the need as a community to support those who for many reasons are not in a position to be able to attain this goal (Cabinet Office 2010, Office 2011, DCSF 2010). This tension between the individual and the community needs is central to the development of societies throughout world history. Different societies find various ways to resolve issues but changes in population size, availability of resources, health of population and climate all influence the increase of the tension between the needs of the individual and the community. The socio-economic pressures of earning money and providing food and shelter are fundamental in all societies and also influence the way in which children are viewed. For example, where children are able to contribute to the family income, perhaps through taking on caring roles for younger siblings to enable adults to take up work or through their own employment, the expectations of childhood and education are different. Related to the role of children in society, the importance of play varies from a means of amusement to crucial for children's learning and development.

Culture as a system of shared meaning in a society provides a framework for children's development and priorities for their learning (Perez & Gauvin pp399). Responses of adults to children's engagement in play, conflict, problem solving and learning skills, communicate the relative importance of particular ways to respond. For example, displaying emotions varies between families, cultures and societies which children learn about as they are supported by adults to learn about their place in the group. Increasingly, families are made up of adults with different cultural backgrounds and as such each family develops values, beliefs and relationships which influence their parenting.

As families make decisions about parenting their children, although they will be influenced by a range of perspectives this is more than likely subconscious, and the range of information now available will contribute to parents making individual decisions about the priorities they hold in respect of their child's development. Therefore having individual discussions with families about their values and views about approaches to behaviour is important and can both help parents to make their decisions and to consider how these relate to approaches used in the early years setting.

Developing a setting approach to behaviour

The early years setting is influenced by its local community and the individuals who work in and attend contribute to the values, beliefs and culture of the setting. It is important that, particularly with respect to behaviour, this is a conscious process and not left to chance. Making discussion of behaviour, social development and emotional understanding a natural part of the daily life of the setting helps adults to feel confident and supported in their responses to children's interactions. Also relationships between colleagues and with parents are more likely to be based on consistent approaches and a developing understanding of individual children.

A fundamental principle which may be helpful as a starting point is that children will be given 'best possible chance' to behave in appropriate ways. This will be strongly supported if adults adopt an approach which accepts behaviour as a means of communication, listening carefully and sensitively interpreting children's interactions.

Although routines are an important part of setting life, the regular review of their purpose and effectiveness is essential to ensure they are supporting positive behavioural messages rather than setting up unnecessary conflicts. For example, long waiting times for resources, periods of inactivity, poor access to materials or restricted access to outdoor spaces all have implications for behaviour. Each of these situations will increase the likelihood of behaviour which communicates frustration, inattention, boredom or low levels of involvement.

Routines are often established from an adult perspective such as the need to get all children fed, to another part of the building etc. However, the success or failure of any routine depends on firstly the way in which it is implemented and secondly how it is experienced by the children or individual child. The test of an effective routine is whether it gives children "best possible chance" to respond in an appropriate way. This means taking account of the likely emotions which will be present at the time.

A major part of developing a setting approach to behaviour is building adult knowledge and understanding. This needs to include advances in theory, practice but also more recent areas of research such as brain development.

Brain Development

Most adults find watching babies in their early stages of development fascinating and intriguing. Babies who are only minutes old are already communicating and responding to those around them. They cry in response to discomfort and are soothed by touch and gentle sounds. Most of all they seem to

Learning about others thinking

Learning about our own thinking

actively seek connection with others. They are responsive in the way they react when cuddled, rocked, spoken to or smiled at.

Our understanding of how this is possible and why human babies develop as they do continues to be the focus of much research. As the story unfolds we learn more about the importance of thinking about child development from conception rather than only from birth. We know that a full term baby will be in the womb for approximately nine months and that amazing development takes places during that time. As well as the physical growth there is increasing interest in the development of the brain during this time.

The first stage in the development of the brain is the formation of the neural plate, which is usually about 16 days after conception. The brain cells, which will become neurons, are known to grow at the phenomenal rate of about 250,000 per minute during certain stages of this early development. The neurons are the nerve cells, which send and receive electrical impulses in the brain. As they grow the neurons begin to differentiate and change in order to fulfill particular roles in brain activity. They are then located in the outer areas of the brain according to their future function. The neurons are in need of lots of energy to be effective in their important role. In fact adult level of energy consumption by the brain is reached by the time the child is around two years old. This is nearly doubled by the time the child is three years old. In order to maintain their

efficiency the neurons are supplied with nutrients and supported by glial cells, which are key to the continued functioning of the neurons. By 28 days after conception the brain shape we are familiar with begins to be recognizable. The brain continues to develop rapidly during the first seven months after conception. By this time the majority of the 100 billion neurons needed to form the brain are formed. They are also by this stage appropriately distributed in the different regions of the brain according to their specific role.

The Human Brain

There are four main regions to the physical make up of the human brain. Firstly, the frontal cortex is a particularly significant area. It is understood to be involved in using and making sense of such things as planning, organization and has a key role to play in expressing and understanding emotions. The frontal cortex is a large area of the brain and represents approximately 30% of the whole cortex. Secondly, the temporal cortex, so named because it is the section of the brain which lies by the temples. This region is particularly engaged in language, senses such as hearing and smell. However, it also has some involvement in understanding emotions and in accessing memory. Thirdly, the occipital cortex is found at the base of the brain. This region is virtually exclusively involved in sight and processing visual information. Finally, the parietal cortex at the rear of the brain is engaged in movement, body sensations and in helping to orientate to different situations.

It is possible to consider some key functions which involve particular areas of the brain. But this is not to say that one area has total responsibility for one function or process. A more realistic view is that connections between different areas of the brain bring together a range of information which then leads to specific outcomes.

In some cases such connections between different areas of the brain are thought about as specific systems. An example of where different elements of the brain work in such an interconnected way would be the limbic system. This system is important in processing information to help us to accurately orientate ourselves to our current situation. For example, are we likely to be under threat or do we have any previous experience of this situation which may be helpful to us now. The limbic system includes three main parts of the brain. These are the amygdala, hippocampus and cingulate gyrus. The cingulate gyrus has been found to help in the recognition of emotional and cognitive conflict situations. The amygdala detects fearful or dangerous situations. If a threat is perceived the amygdala triggers our fight, flight or freeze response. These responses will cause a range of changes to our bodies such as, increased heart rate, muscle tension or beginning to sweat. The hippocampus on the other hand is involved in elements of learning and memory. As such its function

relates to storing and retrieving memories of previous experience or learning. This enables previous experience to be used to inform the most appropriate response.

The complexity of how the brain works is hard to envisage, as is the level of specialization of the areas we have described. For example, although the hippocampus is involved in learning and memory it is not the only area of the brain with this function. The cerebellum also has a role to play in learning and memory but in a very specific sense. The cerebellum function relates to complex learning, which over time becomes semiautomatic. This is often related to situations where complex movements are involved but also adjustments are needed based on information received from the five senses. This would include activities like, riding a bike, driving a car or playing the piano. The cerebellum is not just engaged in the movement aspects of this learning but also the sensory input, which informs decision-making involved in fitting the movement to the current situation. In the case of riding the bike this would include being able to adapt posture or effort to maintain balance in a strong wind or against a sudden push.

Scientific Research

The brain and its mechanisms have long puzzled scientists and a major stumbling block has been the difficulty in being able to "see it working." Historically, information was gathered

Emotions change our brain activity

Seeing someone smile changes how we respond

through individuals who had suffered a variety of accidents or brain damage. By exploring the impact that such differences or change in the brain had on functionality ideas and theories have been developed to explain how it may have occurred. More recently scientist and neurologists have been able to extend their knowledge of the brain and its function through a range of different methods. More technology and computer science have had a dramatic impact on the ability to trace activity in the brain. Being able to complete these investigations without surgery or discomfort to the individual has transformed the process. Further, being able to use smaller, lighter and more flexible equipment has also meant that even very young children can take part without causing them discomfort. In the case of children another key factor is that modern equipment no longer requires that the individual remains absolutely still during the process.

There are several examples of such advances in neuroscientific technology. Particular advances in understanding have been brought about by equipment which allows activity in the brain to be identified as it is happening in response to particular tasks. Two specific examples of this are the functional magnetic resonance imaging (fMRI) and the electroencephalograph (EEG).

The functional magnetic resonance imaging (fMRI) is a scan similar to magnetic resonance imaging (MRI). However the fMRI is able to show the actual blood flow and levels of oxygenation, which are present in the brain at specific times. This flow of blood and varying levels of oxygen indicate which areas of the brain are currently most active. The electroencephalograph (EEG) is similar in that it enables detection of levels of activity in the brain. However, rather than blood flow and oxygen levels the EEG records the electrical impulses generated in particular areas of the brain.

These techniques have enabled much more detailed exploration of the way in which different areas of the brain connect, interact and combine. These scientific enquiries has led to a greater understanding of how the brain is able to gather and process information, as well as instigate action and responses.

Understanding the brain is clearly informed by this new access to information about the workings of specific areas and regions of the brain. However, the full story of the functions of the brain is not just about physical structures and designated areas. A range of chemicals, in particular hormones, further complicates the picture. A variety of hormones are released into the body in response to specific signals and each contribute to different effects. A central part of the brain involved in the process of releasing hormones is the hypothalamus. This part of the brain sends messages to the pituitary gland, which in turn regulates hormone release. Through this process the hypothalamus helps to regulate a range of states such as our feelings of hunger, thirst and temperature.

Research continues to unravel the way in which hormones combine and impact on our responses to everyday or occasional events. However, certain hormones have been found to have an important impact on the way we both feel and react in certain situations. For example, levels of oxytocin in mums who have just given birth have been linked to maternal responses to the baby and the production of breast milk. It has also been suggested that the release of oxytocin may encourage nurturing behaviour such as cuddling and stroking (Robinson, 2003 p64). Another hormone, which continues to be investigated, is cortisol. This is commonly known at the 'stress hormone' and has been found to be a useful tool in understanding changes in stress levels in individuals. The release of cortisol is triggered by the amygdala, which we saw earlier was instrumental in the fight, flight or freeze response to situations judged to be threatening.

Once the threat has been dealt with the levels of cortisol will decrease again, the time this takes varies and is related to differences in the individual's 'usual' levels of stress. Consistent, intense and prolonged high levels of stress and therefore cortisol have been highlighted as having an adverse impact on general health.

During Pregnancy

Pregnancy involves a range of significant changes to the mother's body as the baby grows and develops. A baby normally spends a full nine months in the womb and as we have said the brain is rapidly developing during the majority of that time. By the seventh month the brain structures are fully formed. However, a further consideration is the experience of the baby prior to birth, but once the brain is functioning. The baby is able at this stage to react to changes in sensory experience. For example, we know that babies will respond to sounds and light while still in the womb. Interestingly, they will respond differently to the sound of their mother's voice as opposed to other adults. Unsurprisingly, the baby will also be influenced by the emotional state of the mother. The release of a range of hormones will impact on the developing baby as well as the mother's body. In the normal sequence of events there will be an ebb and flow of a variety of hormones, some in response to the pregnancy and some because of the emotional experiences of the mum. Both mother and baby will be able to accept these changes and the influence will be purely temporary.

Obviously, given the intertwined relationship of the mum and baby during pregnancy it makes sense that a healthy diet and lifestyle will also be important to the baby's development. However, not every pregnancy develops in an ideal context and a range of substances can have specific detrimental effects on the development of the brain. Even in the fully formed adult brain chemicals such as alcohol or drugs will impair brain functioning. For example, alcohol has been linked to difficulties in the ability to communication and processing of meaning. On the other hand, the effect of Ecstasy has been found to flood the brain with serotonin. This then results in the links between neurons closing down (Greenfield 2000). As explained previously the neurons are the specialist nerve cells in the brain. The dangers for the baby's developing brain will of course be all the greater. Such substances are also more likely to have long lasting impact on the functions and in some cases the structure of the developing brain. During the process of building the brain as with any structure is fragile and more susceptible to outside influences than once fully formed.

It is not only consciously introduced chemicals which can have harmful effects on the brain as it grows. A further concern during the early stages of brain development is the impact of particularly high levels of natural substances such as the stress hormone cortisol. While normal levels will rise and fall and be tolerated by both mum and baby, consistent high levels over an extended period of time are likely to have a detrimental effect on the developing brain. For example, the body becomes used to constant high levels of cortisol so is always "on the alert" and "ready for action" rather than having periods of restfulness and relaxation. This constant state of readiness not only makes organs in the body work harder than would normally be necessary but also means that if a new threat is perceived then the levels of cortisol are increased even further. In reality this is likely to lead to an 'over – reaction' to a perceived threat.

In summary, before birth the baby is already experiencing and responding to a range of stimuli. The brain in particular is growing and developing very rapidly. Specific areas of the brain are being differentiated for the special part they will play in the complex functions required for creating a thinking and feeling human being.

Let us assume that the pregnancy goes well and the baby is healthy active and the brain development has followed the expected development journey. By the time the baby is born there will be expected to be about 100 billion neurons in place in the brain. This rapid growth does not stop at birth but continues for several years. This rapid growth means that the brain will virtually double in size over the first two years of the baby's life. This growth is not now about increasing numbers of neurons as before. The main growth is now focused on building connections between the neurons. Incredibly, every new experience the baby has is likely to lead to physical changes in brain. Pathways develop in order to make connections between neurons. These connections allow the transmission of electrical impulses which activate different areas of the brain. This process enables the brain to coordinate appropriate responses to the range of stimulation received particularly from the five sense of touch, sight, hearing, taste and smell.

The baby at this stage is, as described by Maria Robinson (2003), "Primed for survival but not yet (for) living." In order to continue to survive the baby needs to engage an adult carer to look after, protect and provide for them. As a vulnerable baby they are unable to feed themselves, keep warm or protect themselves against danger. They are not however totally helpless. Even a newborn is able to signal if they are in distress or at ease. The mother or main carer soon begins to understand the varying cries of the new baby. Specific crying will probably be recognized firstly as indicating, hunger or discomfort. But it will not be long before parents tune into the more subtle messages such as liking to be held in particular ways. Once the baby is able to secure the attention and engagement of key adults, their chances of survival and ability to thrive are significantly increased. The adults and baby begin their shared journey of discovery of finding out about each other and building their relationship.

Most of all in terms of brain development babies are born with an enormous capacity for and competency in learning. As their learning takes place new experiences gradually become familiar patterns of response. In the brain itself the connections between neurons become more effective transmitters of the electrical signals. This process is known as myelination. In practice the repeated transmission of electrical impulse between neurons begins to establish well-worn pathways between those neurons which work together. These electrical signals are able to travel at a staggering 250 miles per hour along these connections. As this process continues and the number and efficiency of the connections increases the brain begins to develop unique patterns of these neural pathways.

Learning about smiles

Look, listen and note

Through this process the brain is shaped by experiences but also shapes experiences. For example, returning to the example of cortisol, a baby who is regularly left to experience high levels of stress by not being fed when hungry will have consistently higher levels of cortisol circulating through their body and brain. These higher levels of cortisol will be maintained as the body continues to signal it is hungry. If this pattern continues increasing hunger will trigger further cortisol being released and more intense stress being experienced because of the previous experience of lack of appropriate response to the hunger signals.

Emotional Development

As the brain develops the patterns of communicating the body's needs and those needs being met patterns of the rising and falling hormone levels become the norm for the individual baby. For babies, the adults around them are responsible for moderating their stress levels; they are not at this early stage of development able to do it for themselves. Patterns of regulating the baby's emotional signals are developed by the parents as they recognise the likely reasons for the baby crying or being at ease. As adults engage in the relationship with the baby they learn about the individual differences between this baby and any other they have known. Even at this stage some babies will generally appear more fractious or more at ease than others.

These differences will impact on the response of the parent as they also establish patterns and norms of meeting the babies' needs. This will involve varying experiences of prolonged crying for the baby as they communicate their current internal state. In terms of the hormone release and brain function this will be experienced as varying levels of a range of hormones.

This very functional description of how the brain operates can give the impression of the process relying purely on very predictable actions and reactions. However, this leads to the complication which is probably best referred to as a distinction between the brain and the mind. Although there are obvious similarities between individual's brains the minds that are created within them are unique. In development terms, we can think about the brain as the structure and the mind as the personalization of the connections and thinking, which happens within the structure. In real terms it is very hard to separate out the functionality and the thinking especially when actions become semi automatic, habits and familiar responses become characteristic ways of responding.

One of the challenges in working with young children is not to either over or under estimate the thinking that is taking place as such development occurs. In the early stages of development each experience is taking place for the first time. Unlike adults, babies and young children have not yet built up a stock of similar experiences to compare and guide their responses. Although there is meaning in what they do young children are not yet making conscious decisions about their actions or responses.

Importantly, it takes many repetitions of an experience in similar and different circumstances before we have any real sense of familiarity. Associations begin to build and connect experiences. For example, the comforting sense of a familiar cuddly toy with its smell, feel and link to a soothing song from mum as the baby falls asleep. These associations take time to build up into an expectation that one is linked to another. It is a long time before a sufficiently comprehensive concept of the situation is understood to be able to allow for a conscious choice of response being available. Initially it will be more likely that the children are working on the principle that there is only one way to respond until chance and experience opens up other possibilities.

The process becomes increasingly complex as connections between different experiences are brought together and begin to impact on individual's responses. For example, if early experiences of interactions with adults are supportive and positive then seeing an adult approach is most likely to be met with a positive reaction. However, as the baby's social circle increases they will encounter adults who respond in different ways and wariness can be detected. This can be recognized as the baby perhaps looking to the main carer for reassurance before engaging with some adults.

The same will be true of novel experiences where the baby or young child has no previous experience to inform their response. They will look to their familiar adult to ensure that the situation is safe and that they should proceed. This example begins to show how the different areas of the brain can impact on the responses adults observe. As a baby, the most important function of the brain is to ensure survival. This involves securing nourishment, warmth, comfort and safety. To increase the chances of survival the baby needs to connect with a more mature human being to provide for those basic needs. This does not happen overnight, but it is part of a period of rapid development and learning.

This is the time when the connections in the brain are being built and consolidated through mylenation. In order for this to occur the baby and young child needs to have access to an environment, which offers opportunities for learning as well as encouragement to explore. Without this scaffolding of their learning and extension of understanding and communication there is a danger that learning will have a narrow and repetitive focus such as has been found in children deprived of appropriate adults to care for them.

The Graham Allen report brought this impact on brain development sharply into focus by using an image of two 3 year olds' brain scans. One had been appropriately stimulated and cared for but the second had not experienced these positive

Individual differences

Different experiences different understanding

responses and interactions. The striking difference which quality of care makes to young children's development was obvious in the different sizes of the two brains depicted in the scans. As mentioned earlier the rate of postnatal growth is very rapid, with the brain expected to double in size during the first two years, increasing its weight by about 400%. This had occurred for only one of the children whose scan appeared in the Allen report. For the second, although the brain structure was in place the lack of sensory stimulation and experience had drastically reduced the connections and pathways which had been built up between different areas of the brain. This deprivation had also led to some abnormalities in the development of, particularly the cortex and limbic areas of the brain. This may go some way to explain the research findings which show that although children's physical and cognitive growth may be able to 'catch up' after a poor start their social development is likely to continue to be impaired (see Dunn 2004 p120).

Psychology and Neuroscience

There is on-going debate in neuroscience and research about the way in which areas of the brain work together or have separate specific functions. A particular area of interest is in examining how an individual's social understanding develops. Two disciplines, psychology and neuroscience continue to make advances in our knowledge. This is not without controversy however, and criticisms have been levelled at social neuroscience saying that the focus is on reducing the complexity of relationships to simplistic neural responses (Ward, 2012 p7). A more realistic description would be that both psychology and neuroscience are adding to our understanding of how the brain works. Together the different approaches can provide evidence which confirms and refutes hypotheses and so contributes to the gradual unravelling of the puzzles of the human brain and our social understanding.

Conditions for growth

Our particular area of interest in this book is the development of young children's behaviour. Firstly, the idea of behaviour has to be understood to mean the full range of responses which a child (or adult) may produce. It is not just a negative term meaning inappropriate behaviour. A baby's behavioural response to being touched could be either reaching to the source of that touch or flinching away from it. Both responses can be described as behaviour and neither is good or bad. The context in which we observe the behaviour may contribute to our

understanding of why the baby may respond in the way he/she did but does not, of itself, enable us to make a judgment about the behaviour being good or bad.

In developmental terms, a child's understanding of acceptable and unacceptable behaviour emerges from experience and observation of a range of social interactions. From birth the provision of warm, sensitive and loving attention offers a secure and predictable context for children's learning about behaviour. It has been suggested that these relationships have a specific impact on the development of the frontal cortex (Schore, 1994). This being an area of the brain whose growth takes place mainly after birth.

Being physically present, offering food, heat and nappy changing however is not enough to create a positive experience or optimum brain development. The essence of nurturing a child is much more subtle. Even in those very early relationships a baby can detect if the adult is 'in tune' and being responsive to them. Research by Colwyn Trevarthen (2001) and colleagues have identified that a baby will only remain engaged if the adult's interactions are sensitive to their changes in interest and emotional state. If they are out of sync however the baby's facial expression changes from engagement to boredom and in some cases disgust.

A baby then, although not yet able to use language to facilitate thought about the facial expressions, emotional mood or tone of an interaction, will still use a behavioural response to communicate their dissatisfaction in the adult response. When all goes well and the baby experiences more 'tuneful' than 'out of tune' interactions, then they are beginning to build positive experiences of what interactions can be like. It is likely that such early experiences are also the building blocks for future understanding of empathy and recognizing other's emotions. This sense of someone being 'in tune' with you and responding sensitively continues to be valued through out our lives.

This engagement with others develops in a variety of ways such as mimicking, patterns of response being triggered for particular adults etc. A notable development is in the use of pointing which is usually first used in sharing attention in an object with an adult. For example, pointing to a favourite toy or an interesting sound. It is also used as a means of triggering engagement but without a common object/focus. Where adults are not tuning into the child and their intentions this can be misinterpreted as 'just pointing' without meaning. Such a lack of response and understanding may well leave the baby frustrated and engender a need to find more effective ways to attract and engage others.

Seeking to understand the baby's and young children's behaviour in a context of them being competent and skillful learners is much more likely to lead us to reciprocal and responsive interactions. These sensitive and caring interactions which 'tune into' each individual child help adults to create appropriate conditions for healthy brain development and social understanding.

Children learn from those around them, they watch, copy, amend and combine in unique ways the vast range of actions, responses and behaviours which take place around them. It is a very effective way to learn but it is not totally indiscriminate as it may sometimes seem. From a survival perspective it is reasonable to speculate that the child will focus on actions and responses which are shown to be important by those bigger than themselves (i.e. have been around longer therefore must be doing something right to survive!). An example would be the way in which toddlers when first on the move will pick any object up and hold it to the side of their head and make sounds which increasingly sound like "hello". In the context of watching and learning from those around them this is likely to be because of the frequency with which they have observed everyone picking up mobile phones, holding to the side of their heads and making noises into it. From a survival perspective this may well look like something very important because everyone does it with high levels of frequency therefore must be important to know in order to succeed in this environment.

This begins to show how children may be building their understanding of how the world works. The phone example is a very simplistic one but a similar process contributes to social and behavioural learning. If the way in which family members talk to each other demonstrates respect, sensitivity and understanding this will establish a pattern of expected responses and ways of behaving which are important. Given that most children these days spend a significant amount of their week in some form of childcare if the same patterns and values are communicated there too then the message is strengthened.

More specifically, some characteristics of conversations which go on in families has been shown to be supportive of children developing their understanding of other's thinking. Enabling children to engage in talk about how situations or actions have made them feel and to compare different interpretations seems particularly helpful. For example, retelling a conflict situation which had happened earlier in the day including reflection on their own and other's actions. Hearing such a conversation without feeling the immediate emotion is likely to allow more detailed thinking. In the explanation there is scope for talking about each of those involved and to consider how they may have felt. There is no right or wrong answer but the opportunity to try out possibilities and to talk openly about why each of the players reacted the way they did gives practice in seeing things from different perspectives.

This perspective taking is a key skill in successful conflict resolution but also in empathy and friendship. This skill can be supported through a variety of situations that allow for 'safe rehearsal' of the possibilities. For example, using puppets, photo stories and storybooks. Talking through real life situations is particularly helpful but needs to take place once the emotional responses have been given time to subside. This is linked directly with the impact on the functioning of the different areas of the brain in a highly charged situation. If a threat has been detected then the limbic system will trigger the fight, flight or freeze response.

In this situation it is very difficult to engage in complex thinking about why the threat is there the whole focus is survival. Any thinking will be more usefully done at a later stage when the levels of adrenaline and cortisol have subsided and the brain is free to access more complex thinking. This would include being able to remember previous similar events, reflect on the effectiveness of responses and imagine alternative ways for future response. It is important to remember that even as adults we can talk through a range of possible alternatives with appropriate justifications but that is no indication that we will be able to implement them next time round.

Developmentally important understanding

The impact of emotions can be strong and fast, impeding our thinking and suspending our comprehension of a situation. As a young child when each situation is experienced as a new combination of emotions and sensations this can frequently be overwhelming. At the point of being overwhelmed a sensitive, calm and 'tuned in' adult can be instrumental in helping the child to gradually regain control and feel safe. In addition, children will often attempt to learn about dealing with emotions by watching others or acting out situations through pretend and role play. Trying out how it feels to throw things and bang about

Learning to behave

Alongside and engaged

when you are angry in a pretend or role play context can provide an opportunity to see other's reactions and imagine how other's might feel if they are reacting in that way.

Helping children to begin to recognise the physical difference emotions make to their bodies is an integral part of the process of learning to identify emotions. The link between brain activity and hormonal release has specific effects such as, butterflies in your tummy, clammy or sweaty hands, muscle tension or tears. These feelings can be early warnings of emotions and gradually over time understood as an indicator of particular emotions.

Linking these sensations to appropriate facial expressions is an interesting part of the process. As an individual we are able, with practice, to identify those physical changes but our facial expressions are a different matter. We would normally only see these from the inside, not as seen by others. Even given the opportunity to look in a mirror does not give an accurate image of the real emotion we were feeling before the mirror was produced. Photographs are probably the nearest we can get to seeing our own facial expressions of particular emotions but even then there will be a delay in being able to match the two.

One of the benefits of linking these sensations with the facial expressions is that it offers an opportunity to recognise another's internal state and to have an emotional reaction

to some one else's situation. This builds on the ideas of understanding another's perspective and developing empathy.

The concept of being able to 'stand in someone else's shoes' is seen to be important because it enables social connections and friendships. But empathy is also recognized as influential in moderating individual behaviours. For example, the support for this argument would be that if you understand how it feels if someone is unkind to you, you are less likely to be unkind to others. However, this is only part of the story. Our feelings of empathy as adults are dependent on a range of more subtle factors. These would include our previous experience or opinion of the person or the particular context in which the event occurred.

For children their understanding of intentions and motivations take a considerable time to be established. The combination of previous experience of the particular situation or of the individual involved will be likely to be a strong influence. For example, the last time Bobby came near me he hit me or the last time we all ran for the bikes Aleisha pushed me out of the way. The adult influence on child's development of realistic interpretations of the intentions of others, particularly in early years provision is an important part of scaffolding social understanding.

The first possibility is to leave the child to work it out for themselves, depending on their experience and ability to reflect

Do you see what I see?

Do you think what I think?

on the major influences. Particularly for children who are just beginning to interact independently the picture they build from experience could provide a very shaky foundation for this important understanding. For example, interpreting accidental trips or bumps as deliberate pushes could become a pattern which is difficult to change. An alternative is to use a 'reframing' approach in which the adult is able to make explicit a different but realistic intention. For example, Bobby was trying to get your attention to play or Aleisha tripped on the mat.

By using opportunities which arise naturally in the child's interactions it is possible to open out others' thinking and give insights into the range of intentions which may exist. It also ensures that the learning is happening in real life situations and it can be reflected on at a later time. This process models with the child the way in which they can reflect on previous experience and select the most appropriate interpretation. Fundamentally, it also uses the adult experience and thinking to extend the range of possible intentions available for the child to select from. As the child's understanding increases there is also an opportunity for exploring why a particular intention was more likely in one situation than another.

Making sense of the world is a major task for young children and it's complexity is difficult for us to grasp, especially in the context of such rapid changes in brain development during the

early years. Relationships and social connection are integral to individual well-being. This is not to say that everyone needs to be with lots of people all of the time. Rather, it is about the adaptability to be able to relate to others in groups of varying sizes as well as individually with appropriate levels of intimacy. To achieve this it is necessary to be able to make sense of our own and other's behaviours and the ways in which emotions, previous experience and context will influence them.

The process of developing an understanding of other's but also of self is slow and complex. Children have many different opportunities and ways of progressing this thinking but seldom consciously. Their experiences gradually build a picture of how the world works in terms of interactions with both adults and their peers. Patterns of familiar responses begin to emerge and characteristic ways of interacting develop.

We are a long way from fully understanding what takes place and why but technological advances have given us access to more detailed and informative evidence of developmental progress.

This is an ongoing process and no doubt the concepts explored in this section will be further clarified and refined in the near future. However, the implications for current early years practice are clear in that firstly, good quality provision can make a significant difference to the early brain development

POINT FOR REFLECTION

- In what ways does your setting provide a nurturing and supportive environment for healthy brain development?

- Which sources of information have you recently explored to extend your knowledge and understanding of brain development?

- What are your colleagues views of these sources?

- In what way have you changed your practice in response to your learning about early brain development?

- Which observations of children have confirmed your new learning about early brain development?

- In what ways does your understanding of brain development help you to positively support the parents of children you are working with currently?

As practitioners build on their knowledge and understanding they are also likely to be feeling more confident in their discussions with each other. The opportunity to share and compare observations as well as interpretations with colleagues is an important part of extending professional confidence. Questioning ourselves and others about the thinking behind their views is an important skill which will extend our thinking. Making time for sharing ideas and reflections about information from a range of sources helps to refresh our thinking about the individual children we are working with at the moment.

If practitioners in a setting continually invest in their own professional development in a variety of ways they are more likely to be able to support parents too. In particular, sensitively sharing knowledge of child development as it is relevant for the parent and child can really help to support parents' confidence.

As we have said previously, being a parent is a very difficult job and at times can feel very overwhelming. Having an approachable practitioner who also cares about my child to talk through worries and concerns is a valuable support. It is even more helpful if the practitioner is able to bring together a range of knowledge and understanding which helps the parent to have realistic expectations and to feel confident in the approaches they are taking.

of young children. More specifically, the individual interactions that practitioners have with children will be instrumental in their developing understanding of what relationships feel like and how they work. It is the responsibility of practitioners to engage with each child as an individual and to gain insight into their unique understanding of their world.

From this perspective practitioners will be best placed to be an advocate for the child and to appropriately scaffold their social and behavioural learning.

KEY POINTS IN RESEARCH AND THEORIES ABOUT BEHAVIOUR

- Different theories are developed by researchers who are also influenced by their own individual experiences and cultural norms

- Most theories currently popular are more influenced by Western European or American cultures

- No one theory currently explains satisfactorily the complexity of young children's behavioural learning and development

- An awareness and understanding of a variety of theoretical approaches helps to see children's developing behaviour in different perspectives, which can deepen our understanding and enable us to support them more effectively

- It is unlikely that any one theoretical approach will satisfy your curiosity about children's behavioural learning. Talking with colleagues about different theories in healthy debate is a useful tool in our own learning

Chapter 3

Thinking about social learning

An important part of early learning is about being with other children, responding to a range of adults and beginning to understand their own thinking. Making social connections and being able to interact successfully in a group situation are complex processes. Finding a balance between our own and others' needs being met is complicated and different in each relationship. As with all areas of learning, it is inevitably harder for some to grasp than others. The context in which the interaction takes place will generate a range of emotions too. Some places give rise to higher levels of anxiety. For example, children may experience less underlying anxiety in familiar rather than unfamiliar places. Children learn about the ebb and flow of relationships from those around them as well as when they are taking part themselves. They, as do we, watch how people react to each other and to situations. Crucially, direct interactions when they are key players involves dealing with emotional responses, intentions and motivations which require rapid and complex thinking.

However, it is important to note that observing interactions between others also involves emotional responses and trying to workout intentions and motivations, but the observer does not generally have the same pressure to respond immediately. Whilst neither of these situations is easy or straightforward in the thinking and understanding needed, being an observer does give the opportunity to think without being a direct player in the action.

At the early stages of learning about relationships and interactions most of the understanding is at an intuitive level. It is therefore not consciously thought about, verbalised or reflected on, but relies on the feelings which are present. Interestingly, adults who have had many years to practise often continue to find it difficult to verbalise and explain why some relationships work more easily than others. Phrases such as 'she or he understands me' or 'I just knew what you meant' and 'we were so in tune, thinking the same things'

Looking for connections

Can you see the world through my eyes?

are attempts to sum up how it feels when a relationship or interaction works well and is mutually satisfying.

Throughout our lives we find it is easier to get along with some people than with others. However we do have to interact with people even if we would not choose them as our best friends. To achieve this we need to understand that others think differently from us and that our interpretation of their actions will influence our response to them. Essentially, we also have to recognise that our interpretation of their motivations and intentions may not accurately reflect what they are actually thinking. Fundamentally, we have to recognise that our interpretation of their intentions and motivations are mainly guesswork built on our personal experience of the individual and people like them.

Social competence

Even though the process of taking part in an interaction is very complex, with many opportunities for misunderstandings and mistakes in interpretation, most children are able to develop relationships which are mainly successful. Remember, successful does not necessarily mean always happy, easy or positive. Research by Rose-Krasnor (1997) exploring definitions of young children's social competence suggests that there are four general approaches which have previously been taken. Firstly, identifying specific key skills such as recognition of facial expressions. These key skills can be learned through training programmes, observed and recorded. However, being able to demonstrate such skills in isolation does not guarantee their appropriate use in real life play situations. Secondly, using measures of popularity with peers as an indication of high levels of social competence. This approach ignores situations where children are skilful in their interactions and have successful relationships but in a negative and troublesome way. There are many ways to gain popularity or status in a peer group such as getting others to do what you want, knowing how to wind people up, 'buying' alliance through fear or favour. These skills are not negative of themselves, in fact many are necessary leadership skills, but it is the intention and motivation which underlies them that dictates if they are viewed as virtues or failings. Thirdly, social competence can be judged according to the ability to maintain relationships, but again this would not be sensitive to the characteristics of the relationship. Finally, some researchers have examined social competence as the ability to be able to achieve certain social goals, such as completion of a task or game. However, this does not recognise the likelihood of there being more than one possible goal. For example, 'success' for one participant in the relationship may be

POINT FOR REFLECTION

Consider the children you are currently working with and the information in this chapter about definitions of social competence.

- Which children would you describe as socially competent?

- What have you observed that leads you to think of them in this way?

- Which children do you think of as less socially competent?

- What have you observed that leads you to think of them in this way?

In thinking about ways in which you can support children's social learning use the following prompts to inform your observations, discussions with parents and plans for children's learning.

- In which different ways do they approach others?

- Which are their most successful interactions?

- Which other children are they most at ease with?

- Why might this be?

As a staff group what would you consider observational evidence that a child was 'socially competent'?

Think about the following prompts to reflect on what you might see as children play together.

- Ways to join others' play

- Showing understanding of others' thinking

- Recognising own and others' emotions

- Noticing changes in the mood of the group or individuals involved in the play

- Sharing

- Making offers of help to others

LINKS WITH YOUR PRACTICE

It is easy to think of social learning as something that children just get on with by themselves. It is, however, a major part of our lives as human beings to make connections with others and to find ways to maintain relationships. It is not reasonable to expect all children to feel at ease in groups of the same size. Some will be most able to engage with a small number of intimate friends, while others will prefer being part of a much larger group. There is no ideal or 'one size fits all', but it is important that children are able to take part in groups and interact in a variety of situations. Observing children at play is likely to provide the most information about a child's confidence and understanding of social interactions. In a peer play situation children will be most self-reliant and demonstrate their 'real-life' skills of social competence.

Parents as well as practitioners will regularly observe and notice changes in the ways children organise and take part in play situations. Together it is possible to recognise new skills and confidences which the child develops as described in the previous points for reflection bullet points.

An important part of helping children to gain such skills is by demonstrating them as adults and giving opportunities for children to practise and rehearse them. A first step to making this a feature of everyday practice is to review daily routines such as:

- Snack time, especially offering and receiving drinks and snacks from each other

- In focus activities with an adult inviting children to join the group

- During games giving praise, making supportive comments, noticing skills and effort

- When resolving conflicts, adults using language which helps children work out solutions

- Considering opportunities for older and younger children to be together and encouraging recognition of gaining skills with maturity and practice

Each of these situations can be used to provide powerful positive message about ways of interacting.

to fail at the task in order to gain approval from another. To try to bring together and consider the roles of each of these aspects of social competence, Rose-Krasnor developed a model which depicts how, when they come together and are fluently used in real life situations, then, effectiveness in interaction, is the most accurate definition of social competence.

Friendships

As human beings we are undoubtedly interested in making connections with others and this is reflected in the importance we attach to friends and relationships. When young children first attend a setting with other children, be it day nursery, pre-school, childminder, school or holiday club, one of the first questions which arises concerns the child making friends. Friendships are a major feature of adult conversation about young children's early development. In early years this is a particular issue because it is often the first time children make independent relationships outside the family. One of the aspirations parents often mention they have for their children is that they will have friends. This milestone of children making independent friendships seems to tell us that everything will be okay. The child has a companion who will help and support them through the difficulties ahead. Given this level of importance, what do we understand about friendship and its characteristics? Guiding realistic expectations about friendships for children and parents is an important part of practitioners' communication about social development.

Considering what we mean by friendship is a useful beginning to understanding what we are expecting of young children. Children as young as eighteen months (Hay 1994, Dunn 2004) have been shown to have a preference for spending time with specific individuals and to have a shared connection. Connections with others range from a shared experience, however brief, to some form of shared meaning, an understanding that those involved are thinking about the same things and contributing to each other's understanding. Such connections are the basis for children's learning about their own and others thinking. This learning involves the recognition that each person thinks, that they each may be thinking different things and that this thinking will inform their reactions and responses to events.

As discussed earlier, our idea of what others are thinking, or their intentions, may not always be correct. For young children the way in which adults are able to open out others thinking is likely to be a useful way of scaffolding their learning. For

Example: Mediating children's interactions

Being ready to help when needed

Childminder

Jamila, an experienced childminder, became aware that the three year old and two year old she was looking after were getting frustrated with each other, especially when either one of them was tired. Following some observations she realised that there were two key issues. Firstly, there were certain toys which each child found easier to share than others. Secondly, if either child was tired, sharing became a real focus of frustration and upset. In particular, when John was tired, the two year old wanted his cuddly bunny rabbit, but at other times he was able to share it happily for quite a while. When upset Alexander, the three year old wanted his comfort 'blanky' ,but at other times he was not interested in it and happy for John to carry it around or play with it. Jamila began by talking with Alexander about how much he had learned since he was a baby. She used photographs to talk about past events, situations and favourite toys. She noted different ways the two boys were able to resolve sharing disputes when they were playing together. In addition she noted particular signs that the boys were tired, discovering that John usually rubbed his eyes when he was beginning to feel tired while Alexander tended to stroke his cheek with something soft. She modelled noticing

when each of the boys was showing early signs of being tired by sensitively using phrases such as "Alexander, I wonder if John is tired, he seems to be rubbing his eyes, maybe we could find his rabbit for him to cuddle". Although John was younger, she also talked to him about Alexander feeling tired and needing his 'blanky' and modelled finding it and giving to him. This helped Alexander to recognise the tired feeling and to experience being cared for in the same way he was helping to care for John. At times when the boys were not tired Jamila helped them to try out lots of different ways to share things. For example, taking turns, using sand timers, getting another similar toy, using the toy or equipment together, showing each other what to do with the toy, taking photos of the other child playing with the toy while they waited for their turn, etc.

Pre-school

A pre-school staff team was concerned that parents were constantly asking if their children had 'made a friend yet' when they first started attending the setting. The staff team talked with parents individually, and in small groups, about different kinds of friendships which young children develop, sometimes close and long-lasting, sometimes brief and activity-focused,

Example: Mediating children's interactions

Deciding when and how to intervene takes practice

Childminder

Jamila, an experienced childminder, became aware that the three year old and two year old she was looking after were getting frustrated with each other, especially when either one of them was tired. Following some observations she realised that there were two key issues. Firstly, there were certain toys which each child found easier to share than others. Secondly, if either child was tired, sharing became a real focus of frustration and upset. In particular, when John was tired, the two year old wanted his cuddly bunny rabbit, but at other times he was able to share it happily for quite a while. When upset Alexander, the three year old wanted his comfort 'blanky', but at other times he was not interested in it and happy for John to carry it around or play with it. Jamila began by talking with Alexander about how much he had learned since he was a baby. She used photographs to talk about past events, situations and favourite toys. She noted different ways the two boys were able to resolve sharing disputes when they were playing together. In addition she noted particular signs that the boys were tired, discovering that John usually rubbed his eyes when he was beginning to feel tired while Alexander tended to stroke his cheek with something soft. She modelled noticing

when each of the boys was showing early signs of being tired by sensitively using phrases such as "Alexander, I wonder if John is tired, he seems to be rubbing his eyes, maybe we could find his rabbit for him to cuddle". Although John was younger, she also talked to him about Alexander feeling tired and needing his 'blanky' and modelled finding it and giving to him. This helped Alexander to recognise the tired feeling and to experience being cared for in the same way he was helping to care for John. At times when the boys were not tired Jamila helped them to try out lots of different ways to share things. For example, taking turns, using sand timers, getting another similar toy, using the toy or equipment together, showing each other what to do with the toy, taking photos of the other child playing with the toy while they waited for their turn, etc.

Pre-school

A pre-school staff team was concerned that parents were constantly asking if their children had 'made a friend yet' when they first started attending the setting. The staff team talked with parents individually, and in small groups, about different kinds of friendships which young children develop, sometimes close and long-lasting, sometimes brief and activity-focused, sometimes groups related to a current game or craze. With the children each Key Person used children's photographs to talk about positive attributes and skills which children possessed. Children were given cameras to take photographs of the children they liked to be with for different activities. These were used to make a display about children's thinking about friends and friendships.

Day nursery

As practitioners in the day nursery noticed children playing successfully together, they noted the combination of children and the activity they were involved in. The practitioner joined the children and talked with them about how well they were working together and asked what they liked about the friends they were playing with. As a staff group they used short stories (some in books, others they wrote themselves) to talk about and name characteristics of friends. A central theme was that not all friends have all attributes but some have some of them some of the time. This helped children to have ways of describing their relationships in greater detail. It also triggered discussion with several children about how their emotions or being tired made it harder sometimes to be "my kind self." Another aspect of friendship which the children were interested in, but the practitioners had not previously talked with children

example, saying out loud what we are thinking can both model and give a context for our actions. Such as "I'm wondering if I need to put my coat on in case it rains?" or "I think Josh is very sad, that might be why he took the teddy to have a cuddle."

As children develop understanding about their own and others' thinking, they are increasingly able to make sense of the everyday conflicts which arise about sharing toys, not getting their own way immediately and being on the receiving end of others reactions. However, this is not an easy process, especially as it is in the context of early language development, building independent relationships away from key carers, and being cared for by several unfamiliar adults.

Conflicts

As adults, when we help children to sort out conflicts we are providing evidence to add to their understanding of how the world works. Some fundamental beliefs which support conflict resolution are that, "even if I can't have something immediately I can have it soon," "adults will listen to me and help to sort things out in a reasonable way," "I don't always have to give up what I want," "sharing means giving and receiving something," "sometimes it is harder to share, take turns or end an activity than others." The way in which adults talk about and role model these beliefs will support children to recognise consistency in how their world works

in the setting. Ideally, through discussion and shared observations with parents the same messages are communicated at home and in the setting. If this scaffolding of thinking is not consciously considered by the adults, alternative beliefs may be understood by children. For example, "if I can't have it now I will never get it," "adults are always against me," " sharing means I have to give the toy away, no one else has to give away toys or turns, if I make a lot of noise I will get what I want."

Consistency does not need to mean that things happen in exactly the same way every time, but as children recognise familiar responses they and others get to their actions, the more sense they will make of situations.

Consequences are often thought of as the payment for some inappropriate behaviour. However, consequences can be both rewards and sanctions as they are the result of our actions whether these have been positive or negative. Consistency and consequences together give very powerful messages. If the consequence a child experiences of swearing or spitting is to gain the attention of someone who rarely bothers with them and this happens consistently, the learning could be that this is a very effective action to get much-needed attention. A crucial point when considering consequences is that the individual's understanding is based on their experience not yours. By that I mean, where we may have been terrified to be sent to the Headteacher if we had done something wrong, this was as a

Learning with other children

Learning with adults

Sometimes we can sort it out ourselves

confusing is the situation where the same adult responds differently to the same behaviour on different occasions. As individuals our own responses are influenced by our emotions and will not always be exactly the same. However, to support children's learning effectively we need to bring to a conscious level the response which is most likely to enable their learning.

To achieve this successfully involves thoughtful reflection of our knowledge of child development, the individual child's current understanding and previous learning. To increase the consistency of our response it is essential that we talk with colleagues and parents to decide on the response which will give the child 'best possible chance' of success. This consensus increases confidence in the agreed response and makes it more likely that adults will be more consistent. This will not mean that each adult does exactly the same but they will communicate the same message in a very similar way if the preparation has been detailed enough and is based in realistic expectations of the child's current development and understanding.

A useful part of this type of discussion is to explore why adults feel it is important to address this particular behaviour which the child is presenting. Sometimes we can be distracted from what is really relevant and important to the child's progress to something which is less important.

It can be useful to think about 'primary' and 'secondary' behaviours so that our focus remains consistent. Primary behaviours are the ones we have decided we need to focus on at the moment. Secondary behaviours are distractions which follow our response to the primary behaviours such as the child laughing, 'answering back' or mimicking the adults.

result of our own experience and understanding built up over time both at home and in school. For the child you are working with, their experience may be quite different and lead them to understand different things about such a consequence. For example, seeing the Headteacher could be something which is viewed as funny or unimportant, regardless of the reason, and this may be reinforced by other adults outside the setting.

Supporting appropriate social behaviour is about helping children to experience and recognise when connections and relationships are going well, rather than focussing on when things go wrong. The most confusing situation for a child is when different adults respond in different ways to the same behaviour. Equally

KEY POINTS IN THINKING ABOUT SOCIAL LEARNING

- Learning about social interactions is complex and each relationship is different in the emotions we feel and the reactions we give and receive

- Friendships and social connections are important to an individual's well-being and understanding of self

- Conflicts are inevitable and a natural part of any relationship, helping children to use problem-solving to

work out different ways of resolving difficulties is a crucial part of early social emotional learning

- The way young children see adults and older children respond in interactions gives powerful messages about how relationships work

- Think with colleagues about which are the important 'primary' behaviours which need to be addressed

Chapter 4

Thinking about emotional learning

I can...

and I can too!

There are strong links between our emotions and the way we respond to situations. The emotions we experience change how we look and sound as well as how we interpret what we see and hear. Watching an event when we are feeling relaxed and calm will trigger a different set of responses than if we see the same event when feeling stressed and anxious. In this sense our emotions change our behaviour.

It is important that we think carefully about what we mean by the word "behaviour". A narrow, negative definition limits our thinking. If we only think of the word 'behaviour' as meaning something negative or inappropriate we miss the point that behaviour is a response and a means of communication. If we only think of the narrow negative interpretation, we also reduce our ability to support children's behavioural learning. By accepting the wider perspective that behaviour is everything we say and everything we do, this takes into account the whole

range of both the positive and negative aspects of behaviour. Further, if we recognise that everyone will have individual differences in experience and characteristics which influence their understanding of behaviour, then we can begin to see just how complex the topic of behaviour can be.

Communicating emotions

The role played by emotions in young children's understanding of social interactions has been the subject of much recent research (Halberstadt, Denham, & Dunsmore, 2001). Firstly, the importance of facial expressions as an indication of emotional states. Secondly, the ability of young children to use a range of skills to recognise and respond appropriately to clues about their own and others' emotional state. Halberstadt and colleagues, for example, suggest that sending, receiving

POINT FOR REFLECTION

What are the current approaches in your setting to supporting children's learning about the full range of emotions?

Think about the stories, role play and pretend play situations where children are talking about different emotional responses. In your reflections you may want to consider the following:

- Are all emotions talked about or is it mainly being happy or sad?

- What adult response is most likely to be given to expressions of anger or frustration?

- Does the response to expressions of anger support respect and empathy or does it give the message that being angry is something which is not allowed?

- Which words do children use to describe the emotions between happy and sad, angry and frightened etc?

- In discussion with parents and families are children expressing their emotions in similar ways both at home and in the setting?

Building on your knowledge of individual children it can be useful to think specifically about their understanding of emotions in recognising those who are skilled and those who may struggle. In particular this may give some important insights into difficulties they may be having in social interactions. Reflecting on the following may also be helpful:

- Which changes in facial expression or body language do you notice as individual children's anxiety or frustration increase?

- Are these the same early signs that parents identify?

- For children whose anxiety levels are generally high and therefore may be more sensitive to changes or unfamiliar situations, what is most helpful in reducing anxiety levels. It may be helpful to consider the following possibilities:
  1. Reflecting on similar times when a change or event has turned out to be very positive and happy
  2. Talking through what is about to happen
  3. Talking and showing a sequence of photographs

and experiencing emotions, are important and different aspects of our communication with each other. They also consider that there are four abilities which impact on each of these aspects. These are awareness of, identification and regulation of emotions as well as consideration of the social context in which they occur. Bringing these abilities and skills together, as Halberstadt and colleagues suggest , would enable us to understand that sending emotional signals would include being aware of different emotions, identifying those emotions and being able to regulate the emotions and the signals being sent. The same four aspects would apply in a similar way to receiving and experiencing the full range of emotions. Although the four aspects are not described as hierarchical, it is conceivable that awareness of emotions would have to be at a conscious level before identification or regulation could be achieved.

Our behaviour, including these emotional responses, is then essentially a means of communication. One of the useful points which the work by Halberstadt and colleagues shows is that there is a distinct difference in being able to communicate our emotions effectively and to make sense of emotional communication sent by others. It is obviously just as important to be able to "read" and understand the emotional signal and behaviour of others to enable us to make sense of interactions. The simplest example is to be able to recognise and understand facial expressions. This is not just naming the stylised happy or sad face picture, but being able to recognise facial expressions in real situations so as to respond in an appropriate way. Real life facial expressions are much more complex than the stereotypical pictures. They are therefore harder for children to make sense of, but they are essential clues to whether the interaction with someone is going to be pleasant or not. This will influence feelings of wanting to stay and prolong the interaction or to escape from it. There is obviously an extensive range of individualised facial expressions that signify each of the main categories of emotions i.e., happy, sad, angry and frightened. In addition, of course, there are numerous feelings between happy and sad which have no easily identifiable facial expression. Even though this sounds very complicated, the majority of children can name (or point to), recognise and predict emotional expressions and faces by 18 months and continue to refine this skill as it applies to those they regularly interact with (Buss & Kiel, 2004; Denham, 1986).

'Reading' the facial expression of someone else is different from realising how our own faces change as we experience different emotions. Basically, facial expressions look different from the inside, so children cannot be expected to know

Example: Finding out about emotions

Recognising the emotional signals

Childminder

As a simple activity to begin helping children to be able to build their vocabulary about emotions, Debbie made sock puppets with the three children (3, 4, and 5 year olds) she was currently looking after. To extend the children's thinking she devised simple scenario picture cards such as a child and mum shopping in a very busy supermarket, or an empty play park. Debbie talked with the children using the puppets about different emotions they might feel. For example, in the supermarket scenario one puppet was worried about going into the busy shop, another puppet felt happy to be with mum. In the park situation one puppet was lonely while another delighted to have the chance to use all the equipment on their own. Debbie initiated short discussions with the puppets, but the children could also choose to play with them. She also used the same kind of discussions in real life situations with the children and their parents. Her observations showed that the different words the children used to describe feelings increased over a four week period. She also noted that the 4 and 5 year olds were beginning to comment that the same event e.g. going to the park gave rise to different feelings for them at different times.

Pre-school

The usual practice in Happy Days Pre-school was to make photo books for each of the children about their time at pre-school. The books were available in the book corner for some time to share before children took them home. While sharing a book with a small group of children Nadhu noted that the children were able to remember how they felt in some of the photos. She extended the children's thinking by talking about the differences in their facial expressions in a range of photos. The children used duplicate photos to make collections of photos showing different emotions. One of the new children asked 'What if you are not happy or sad?' This started a discussion about feelings words and the children gathered words to describe the range of feelings between happy and sad. The adults realized that words to describe feelings such as 'happy' or 'sad' were not accurate enough for the children. One of the games the children devised was putting the words in order from happy to sad. This resulted in lots of talk about when you might feel each of the emotions and just how sad or happy it really was. The children's comments were recorded and shared with their parents.

how their face looks when they feel a particular emotion. Therefore the sending aspect of communicating emotions is also a complicated process. Thinking about the four abilities identified by Halberstadt and colleagues, being aware of the emotional signals you are sending requires considerable reflection and thoughtfulness before you are able to skilfully regulate the messages you send.

LINKS WITH YOUR PRACTICE

Individual adults often have quite different views on talking about emotions, which can range from never mentioning them to talking about them all the time. Equally, vocabulary used to name emotions can mean very different things to each of us. Where one person may describe their feelings about a particular event in an understated way, another may describe the same event in a dramatic and even exaggerated manner. Our experience as we grow up strongly influences what we understand to be appropriate in displaying emotions in different situations. The children in your setting and their families will have different views about this, as will each of your colleagues. However, we know that being able to think about and understand our own and others' feelings is important to well being and social development. Therefore in our work with young children we need to find ways to talk about and share ideas about similarities in how people may be feeling and the ways in which they may communicate this to others.

Although it may sometimes be useful to use puppets and stories as the basis for this discussion, using children's real life experiences is also an important part of the process. For example, both children who are involved in a disagreement and those watching will have feelings about their experience. Being able to talk through the shared experience supported by an adult provides a useful opportunity to recognise that each participant will have a slightly different perspective. Where adults are able to open out others' thinking and talk about the variety of feelings someone may have about an event, the richer children's understanding of emotions can become.

Emotions are valuable signals which inform us about our own and others' thinking. In particular they help us to consider the motivations and intentions which lead to specific actions.

Being able to 'read' emotional clues such as facial expressions presumably gives children a better chance of being able to respond appropriately in an interaction. It is also likely to contribute to feelings of empathy and being able to see things from another's viewpoint. The impact of emotional understanding on successful social interactions is clear, in fact it has been found to increase the chances of children being perceived well by playmates (Fabes, Eisenberg, Hanish, & Spinrad, 2001). This also emphasises the point that isolated skills of recognising faces, naming emotions etc, are only a small part of the picture; it is the ability to use this understanding fluently in real life situations which contributes to social competence. A further point to be highlighted is that the range of emotions which children are able to recognise in others and express themselves needs to be wide and varied in order to build understanding. It is easy, but not helpful, to give messages to children that the only acceptable emotions to be expressed are happy and sad. The reality is that we all experience a range of emotions on a daily basis and seldom do they neatly fit into the descriptors happy or sad. Increasing the vocabulary and acknowledgement of different feelings provides a useful basis for gradual learning about appropriate ways to express the full range of emotions. In a context where adults and children regularly talk appropriately about feelings as well as demonstrate empathy and respect for others' emotions it is more likely that children will be able to find suitable ways to show how they feel.

Getting to know individual thinking

Regulating emotions

The regulation of our behaviour is very complex and is influenced by many things including genetics, temperament, family values, cultural norms about emotional display and individual differences in our perceptions. But being able to recognise and predict the early warning signs and signals of others (as well as their own) emotions gives a child greater chance of being able to regulate their own responses in the most effective way. Interestingly, again the children most able to regulate their responses have been found to be viewed as most likeable by their peers (Denham, et al., 2001).

There is an important developmental consideration in this process where children are at the early stages of independence, typically although not always at around two years old. The combination of early language development and frustrations in communicating intentions and the strong desire to do things independently can lead to regularly being overwhelmed by emotions. There is a sense of skills, abilities and understanding being out of sync as children at this stage watch and want to be like those a little more mature who must seem as if they can so much more. The role of the adult in mediating between children at this stage and the situations in which they find themselves is a really important one. Scaffolding children's learning sensitively will contribute to their understanding of themselves as competent learners with the ability to persevere when things are difficult and to give and receive appropriate help. Where the adult acknowledges the children's likely feelings and gives time and space for them to attempt difficult tasks at their own pace but with support when wanted, children are provided with a useful model of regulating emotions to learn from. Giving a supportive commentary of actions allows for recognition that things do not always go well but can still be managed or resolved. Further naming

and acknowledging emotions gives a clear message about empathising and the appropriateness of the feelings. Finding out what it feels like to be sensitively supported to deal with such feelings is an integral part of the process and a key lesson in learning to regulate your own emotions.

A crucial part of supporting children's emotional understanding in early years provision is being able to share observations and interpretations with other adults. This may be mostly with colleagues but, particularly in the case of childminders, also parents. This process enables adults working together to recognise those who are finding it more difficult than others to express their emotions appropriately. From this starting point adults are able to consider times when the child has most success, and to explore together why this might be and identify ways to make it happen more. In particular this will include recognition that this may be temporary because of specific events, developmental or temperamental, and that fundamentally some children will find regulating their behaviour and emotions more difficult than others. As we know, learning is a very individual process and the time and effort required varies considerably in all areas of learning – including and maybe especially, behaviour.

An important approach is to recognise that children are not deliberately setting out to upset people, but are most likely genuinely trying to work out how the world works.

The world is a very confusing place and as language competence and independence increases young children can regularly be overwhelmed by their emotions. In the busy lives of parents it can be particularly hard on some days to hold on to the view that their child is not deliberately setting out to make their lives difficult. A key role for practitioner is to use their knowledge of child development to support parents realistic expectations of their children and to talk about their behaviour in this context.

KEY POINTS IN THINKING ABOUT EMOTIONAL LEARNING

- Emotions and feelings influence the way we behave and react

- Each relationship we are involved in will evoke a unique set of emotions for us

- Being able to 'read' others' emotions through facial expressions, tone of voice and body language,

for example, will help us to gain insights into another's perspective

- Learning about our own and others' emotional responses is a life-long and complex process and young children need lots of help to begin to understand. As part of the learning there will of course be many misunderstandings

Chapter 5

Thinking about behavioural learning

To effectively work with young children and support their behavioural learning appropriately it is essential to share your observations with both colleagues and parents. Everyone has a slightly different perspective and if we rely solely on our own we are less likely to be either accurate or helpful. By listening to parents and colleagues' views we can share the thinking and hypotheses about the intentions and motivations which may be behind the behaviour. For this to be a positive experience and supportive of young children's learning. It needs to happen in a setting culture of respectful engagement with parents. This culture of communication is most likely to develop if colleagues are encouraged to work together to solve problems and reflect on the effectiveness of their practice. From the on-going discussions between parents and practitioners and the cumulative experience of staff teams a general pattern of expectations of children's behaviour develops as part of the setting culture. These expectations will reflect developmental progress, adult professional knowledge about behaviour and general attitudes to children.

Policy and practice

The setting policies, particularly the behaviour policy, will reflect the values, principles and approaches to behaviour which are part of everyday practice. This link between policy and practice is essential. A policy written by one member of staff which is only read once by new members of the team is not likely to improve practice or give an accurate picture of current staff responses. Where the staff team can explain clearly the setting policies and, more importantly why these approaches have been employed will evidence the thought and commitment which has been invested in making

What if we all want to be first?

How do I communicate what I want?

professional decisions. Being able to have such conversations with parents, visitors and colleagues helps the policies to continue to be living documents which will evolve and grow with the professional development of the staff team.

Influences on behaviour

A core part of an effective early years provision is developing realistic expectations of the children's learning and behaviour. The previous chapters give an opportunity to reflect on some of the influences which determine children's behavioural response to interactions and situations. As part of the journey, the idea of individual differences has been highlighted in several ways. Mainly so far, this has related to early experiences and relationships and how they can influence children's expectations of their own and others motivations, intentions and actions. Thinking about the child as an individual, there are other influences on behaviour which are important to consider in order to inform our realistic expectations. An obvious factor is gender. Research by Eleanor Maccoby (1990) suggests that boys and girls may well have different social experiences in their peer play. Research evidence to date indicates that boys tend to play in larger groups and that their play tends to be focused around an activity. Popularity in a group for boys may be more strongly influenced by their ability to demonstrate particular skills, rather than being able to ask nicely if they can play. An example of this would be a boy running alongside a football game in the hope that his skill would be noticed and that he would be invited to join the game. For girls it seems they are more likely to play in smaller, more intimate groups where popularity may depend on being able to establish and maintain relationships with key individuals. This is a possible explanation of the importance of being invited to parties and the "I'm not going to be your friend" challenges.

Although it may seem strange to talk about age in terms of an individual difference, it is worth considering that age is not just about the number of years we have lived, it is also about the cumulative effect of the experiences we have had to date. It is also about recognising the spread of ages which is represented in the group of children with whom we are working. A summer born child in a reception class will quite appropriately be at a different stage of development and maturity than a child whose birthday falls in the winter months for example. Therefore, having realistic expectations is about reviewing our knowledge of the individual child. In this process we will take account of an individual's skills relative to others of a similar age, but also the recognisable progress made over a period of time. 'Stages' is

POINT FOR REFLECTION

Although writing and reviewing policy documents is often seen as an uninteresting and tedious part of the job, it can provide a useful opportunity to talk about and increase everyone's understanding of "how we would like it to be round here". This process of discussion and compiling the policy document also builds individual practitioners' confidence that they are responding to the children and parents in a similar way to their colleagues and have similar reasons for doing so. A further advantage is that for leaders and managers it can contribute to decisions about training needs for themselves, whole staff or individual practitioners. Some of the following may help to contribute to your thinking about approaches to behaviour currently used in the setting.

- How many of the current staff group were involved in writing or redrafting the setting behaviour policy?

- In discussion, what are the range of views expressed by the staff about children's behaviour?

- What evidence do you have that the views are reflected in day to day practice in the setting?

- Which aspects of the policy and practice do you feel happy and in tune with?

- Which aspects of the policy and practice feel uncomfortable or out of sync with your thinking?

- In what ways do the policy and practice show that practitioners try to see things from the child's perspective?

- In what ways do staff give children the 'best possible chance' to learn about behaviour ?

- In what ways do practitioners support each other if a child is presenting challenging behaviour?

- In what ways do practitioners support the child who is presenting challenging behaviour?

- In what ways do practitioners support the parents whose child is presenting challenging behaviour?

LINKS WITH YOUR PRACTICE

A regular part of the life of any early years provision is to consider and update policies to ensure they reflect current practice. It is particularly important to review the messages which are being given about behaviour. If staff and parents are engaged in the development and review of the policies, it is more likely that there will be consistency between the written policy and daily practice. Further, by viewing behaviour as similar to other areas of learning, consistency in approach can be maintained. For example, that children develop skills, knowledge and attitudes at different times and that the adult role is to scaffold learning and build on children's areas of interest and achievement.

As has been highlighted in previous chapters, there are many influences on young children's developing understanding of their own and others' behaviour. But the most important thing to remember is that this is a very complex process which children are generally doing their best to make sense of and understand. From an adult perspective getting to know individual children and being a learning companion provides crucial insights into their current thinking. Listening, not just to the words they use but also to the meaning and thinking they communicate, can help to open our eyes to children's strengths and abilities in a new way.

The time when children are most 'on the spot' in being able to employ their social competence is in a peer play context. While adults may be patient and forgiving most of the time, in the heat and rapid pace of a game children often show little tolerance of each other. This is the context where children demonstrate their 'real life' understanding of social interactions.

When reviewing children's behavioural learning it may be useful to use the following prompts to guide your reflections.

● Which children generally play in large or small groups?

● Which children are most likely to suggest what to play or when to change the game?

● Which children are most able to keep interactions going with others even when there are squabbles or disagreements?

an awkward idea to work with as it suggests that all children will progress through a series of clearly defined and recognisable periods of development at specific ages. This is obviously not the case, although experience working with large numbers of young children does mean that there are some obvious milestones which happen around a similar time for most children such as crawling, walking and talking but even for these there is a broad timescale in which they occur.

Temperament

A further aspect of individual difference not yet explored is temperament. In some cases 'temperament' and 'personality' are used as if they mean the same thing and are linked to an idea that 'it is just the way he or she is.' This implies that the situation is static and unlikely to change. Personality is a combination of characteristic patterns of thinking, reacting, attitudes and feelings which have over time become relatively consistent features of an individual (Atkinson et.al.1990). This is not to say that aspects of personality cannot change, only that patterns of responses usually develop. For example, some people are generally friendly and sociable though they may over time change the groups with whom they prefer to mix. Temperament is considered to be one aspect of personality and has been the subject of considerable research over several decades. A significant contribution to

Who do I feel like today?

Example: thinking about influences on behaviour

Routines and interactions influence behaviour

Childminder

As a regular part of her practice Joleena, who looked after four children (2, 3, and two 5 year olds), began sharing observation with parents about children's emotional state when they were involved in certain activities. Together with parents she built a shared understanding of when children might be anxious, excited, frightened, cross, worried, sad or tearful. The shared knowledge was used to support the children in recognising and naming their feelings. Joleena and the parents together discovered ways to pre-empt some of the children's anxieties. For example, realising that planning a shopping trip resulted in Amelia showing signs of anxiety, her parents worked with Joleena to find ways to help Amelia to see shopping as less unpleasant. They used a series of short trips to a variety of shops to work out what it was about shopping which was causing the anxiety. At first it seemed to be the size of the shop, with supermarkets causing the highest levels of concern. However, further discussion between Joleena and Amelia's parents suggested it was more to do with how busy the shops were. It also helped if Amelia had her own shopping list. Joleena had made several cards with the labels from products which the

family regularly bought. During the shopping trip Amelia was able to use the cards to match with items on the shelf.

Joleena extended this work with all parents to look for 'first signs' of particular emotions, especially anxiety, fear or uncertainty and anger. This helped the adults to support the children and reduce these emotions before they were overwhelmed by them and communicated this through their behaviour.

Pre-school

There were three new members of the staff team at Fun Time Pre-school so the first staff meeting of the term was planned as a focus on behaviour to review and update the setting policy. Rather than just going through the document and changing wording as they had done previously, the team began with trying to explain what the word 'behaviour' meant to them. Some listed things they recognised as signals of 'good' behaviour such as saying please and thank you, playing without hurting, taking turns, doing as asked by an adult, asking an adult for help if their was a conflict. Other members of staff focused on the inappropriate behaviours and felt that the policy should clearly list the sanctions and consequences which would be used if there was an incident of hurting, biting, not doing as an adult asked, etc. A third group began to think about how we learn about behaviour and recognised several influences such as parenting, extended family, friends, older children, television, local community. As each group fed back their ideas, there was useful discussion about the fact that all three perspectives were indeed a part of the meaning of 'behaviour'. Believing that a behaviour policy should be a working and useful document, the team turned their attention to exploring behaviour from a child's perspective. This led them to consider that they, as a team, were one of the key influences on the behaviour of the children who attended. The revised policy then began to take shape as a document which highlighted the behaviours which the staff would demonstrate in order to show the children supportive and effective interactions. This was talked about in the policy in the context of relationships between staff, staff and parents as well as staff and children. From their knowledge of the local area the staff recognised that the children would be coming to the pre-school having had very different experiences of relationships and responses to their behaviour. This led the team to identify key messages which they wanted to give to all children and parents. They recognised that for some children these would be very familiar, for others they would be completely new. Similarities with other areas of learning quickly emerged and helped to inform ideas about realistic expectations of individual children's behaviour. At the end of the staff meeting a draft policy was completed, but the team decided to revisit it after three weeks to see how it related to their experience of the beginning of the new term. They also decided to contact parents of children who had left to seek their views, firstly of how children had settled in school but also what messages about behaviour the parents thought the team had been communicating the previous year.

Day Nursery

Behaviour, or at least inappropriate behaviour was a regular topic of discussion at Marlewood Day Nursery. However, the staff team was concerned that communication with parents seemed to be more about negative than positive behaviours. This was having the effect of both parents and practitioners talking less to each other at the beginning and end of the day in case a behaviour issue was raised. The room leaders and management team talked together about possible ways to redress the balance, but struggled to come up with a specific solution. They invited a couple of parents from each

room to join their discussions. Together they talked about the children's behaviour and how they usually communicated about it. The parents raised the following key points:

- With so much in the news and in chatting with their friends about children's bad behaviour, they were very worried about how their own children behaved when they were not with them

- No one expected their children to be good all the time, but friends understandably talked mainly about their children's achievements and good behaviour and this made it hard to feel confident about your own children's behaviour

- Parenting was not easy and it was hard to feel confident about what were realistic expectations for children's behaviour at different ages and stages

- With so little time to talk at the beginning and end of the day it was necessary to get the "bad" news out of the way quickly

- If practitioners reported a behaviour issue, it was hard to know how to react or what to do to stop the behaviour happening again

- It was very distressing to hear that your child had behaved inappropriately, especially if this involved hurting someone

The practitioners talked about the following as important issues:

- It was hard to know what to say to parents about their child's behaviour

- Most of the children's behaviour was age and stage appropriate and focused on them learning about friendships and how to get along with others

- Issues which occurred during the day were dealt with in the context in which they happened, and for the children to be reminded about it at the end of the day with their parents sometimes made it into more of an issue than was necessary

- Sometimes because it was difficult to talk with parents about their child's behaviour, the discussion didn't happen until it was a much more of a problem

our understanding of temperament has been derived from the work of Mary K. Rothbart (Rothbart, 2011). Her life's work has focused on researching the influences of different aspects of temperament on personality and relationships. Temperament, then, is a word which can be readily used in early years but seldom considered in any detail.

The importance of exploring temperament is to increase our understanding of why some children may find it more difficult to manage their responses to situations than others. Rothbart and her colleagues define temperament as "individual differences in reactivity and self-regulation" (Rothbart & Derryberry 1981). This refers to differences in emotional responses to situations, ability to maintain our attention and levels of physical activity. For example, an individual may have a tendency to be excitable or slow to respond, try to attend to several things at once or persevere in attending to one thing despite distractions, always on the move or generally still. Although everyone will respond in a variety of ways depending on the situation, most of us will tend towards particular patterns of responses. Given this tendency, it is reasonable to accept that for a child who is generally very active it will be harder to be still if required than for a child who is less likely to be so active.

It is fascinating and a privilege to observe and support children's early behavioural understanding. However, it can also be very challenging as some children in particular struggle with strong emotions and difficult interactions. As individuals not only do we have to learn about others and their reactions but also to reflect on our own emotions and how we can most appropriately express them. The reality of working with groups of children is that often it is our behaviour and that of our colleagues which is one of the strongest influences on their responses while they are in our setting. We are, at all times in the setting, role models for the children we work with, this professional responsibility is something we accept

when we are employed. As part of our own professional development building understanding of our own emotional intelligence as well as strategies to regulate our own behaviour is a useful approach to maintaining our professionalism.

In thinking about these aspects of individual differences it is possible to appreciate more fully the range of possible influences on a particular child's behaviour. Given this complexity it is much easier to understand that there is no 'quick fix' or 'one size fits all' response to helping a child whose behaviour gives us cause for concern. In addition there are temporary influences on our emotions which can result in significant changes in our behaviour. For example, children who are experiencing changes or disruption at home e.g., new baby arriving, moving house, parents living apart, new adults living at home etc the emotions they feel are often confusing and difficult to express. Practitioners can work with parents to use knowledge of the individual child's emotional understanding as a basis for agreeing ways to help the child make sense of what is happening. As well as the factual information accepting that conflicting emotions will also be present is important to acknowledge. Although there might be a hope that everything will go smoothly it is more likely that being able to talk openly about some of the negative feelings will help to make new arrangements work better in the long run. For example, a new baby often results in perceived pressure for the older child to be 'a good big sister/brother' 'very grown up' etc. These phrases mean different things to different individuals and can be very scary especially if you would still really like to be cuddled and fed like the baby. Understanding the ways in which the relationship between parent and child have changed as well as how it has stayed the same is difficult to grasp for both older and younger children.

The next chapter explores ways in which we can use effective early years practice to develop a practical approach to supporting the child's learning.

KEY POINTS IN THINKING ABOUT BEHAVIOURAL LEARNING

- Engaging all staff and parents in the review and updating of policies will contribute to a culture of respectful engagement and consistency between policy and day-to-day practice

- Developing realistic expectations of children requires understanding of individual differences such as combinations of temperament, age, stage and gender

- Looking for characteristic patterns of peer play can be helpful in understanding children's current social competencies

- Talking with parents about the progress children are making in their behaviour in the same way as other areas of learning can prevent escalation of difficulties

Chapter 6

Using observation and analysis

What do you see?

Gather parents observations

"Everyone is a genius. But if you judge a fish by its ability to climb a tree, it will live its whole life believing it is stupid."

Albert Einstein

Making observations is a regular part of everyday life in early years settings but in reality we all observe all the time, sometimes consciously sometimes not. We notice things which are unusual, making a 'mental note' of events which we need to return to later. These observations contribute to a bank of knowledge which informs the way we respond to and work with children. This knowledge base is important to build up so that we can tune in more successfully to young children's interests, strengths and levels of understanding. Parents are also engaged in similar observations and mental notes. Parents have a comprehensive and detailed knowledge of their children, gained through observation and interaction over a long period of time. They have seen their children in many different

situations and interacting with lots of different people. Skilled practitioners are able to talk with parents, show how much they value this information and demonstrate how it can positively contribute to the children's development. At the beginning of the relationship between parents and practitioners, one of the barriers can be the relative importance which is attached to parent and practitioner observations. By establishing an equal balance, right from the start parents and practitioners are able to gain insight into different facets of the child's development. This process cannot help but enrich the shared understanding of the child. By regularly asking sensitively for parents' observations of their child, a useful pattern of sharing observations can form the basis of a very productive and equal relationship.

Two observers of the same event will always see things from a different perspective and note similar but different things. They will also interpret their observations slightly differently. A part of the early challenges in getting to know a child well is the way in which different adults interpret their observations of the child's responses. For example, seeing a child slap another could be seen as:

- Deliberately trying to hurt

- Making contact and wanting to join in

- Responding to someone getting too close

- Reacting to someone taking something they are playing with

- Feeling anxious that they will not get a turn at something

- Needing attention

An adult's interpretation will, as we have seen in previous chapters, depend on many things. But as an early years professional your interpretation should give each child the 'best possible chance' to develop their social understanding. In the early stages of getting to know a child this will require giving them the "benefit of the doubt." It will require making the effort to think about situations from the child's perspective. Coming into an unfamiliar situation with lots of new adults and children will be as daunting for most children as it is for adults. Feeling unsure of what will happen and how events will unfold will raise anxiety levels. This increase in anxiety will have an impact on the individual's behaviour and responses.

Interpreting observations

One of the particular dangers to guard against is to read adult thinking into children's actions and to assume that children "know what they are doing." Knowing infers conscious thought and taking time to think through and plan a response. This process does not take into account the emotions which frequently override thoughtfulness. In the majority of cases the young children we are working with are not going through this process in their everyday reactions. Referring to our knowledge of child development and recognising the complexity involved, it is more likely that the child is responding intuitively than reflectively. They are at an early stage of differentiating their thinking and understanding of emotions (Robinson, 2010). In a practical sense, this is the kind of situation to engage parents bringing their in depth knowledge of their child together with the practitioners' understanding of child development.

POINT FOR REFLECTION

- What advice and training have practitioners in the setting already received to support their understanding of young children's behaviour?

- In what ways are your setting observations shared with parents?

- To what extent are parents able to contribute their own observations to children's records?

- Which local links are the most helpful in increasing the confidence of practitioners in using analysis of observations to support children's learning?

Given the previous chapters in this book, there are some things which are worth considering in working with children with additional needs.
For example:

- With any SEN or diagnosis there is an impact on a child's social connections

- Children may be more inclined to talk to an adult near by rather than directly to the child themselves i.e., Does he like milk?

- The danger of too much adult support is that the child does not get enough opportunity to make independent connections with other children

- Finding a balance of social experience which suits the individual child and contributes to their well-being, including, time on their own, with small group of peers, one friend, several friends, large group of peers, with an adult, with a group and an adult

- Building confidence in developing awareness of their own needs and to recognise feeling of calm, competence, excitement, enthusiasm, connection, independence, autonomy etc

- Developing strategies which work by pooling knowledge and understanding from the child themselves, adults with different perspectives of the child at home, setting, and other professionals

Pointing...

Finding the way out...

Regular sharing and questioning of interpretations of observations with colleagues is a key part of this process. It enables the exploration of a variety of possible interpretations before settling on the current most likely one. Question and challenge are crucial to avoid adults colluding with each other to build a negative consensus.

Whilst the negative consensus will lead to the child being seen as a problem, the positive challenge approach is more likely to lead to joint problem solving.

Through this process adults are also developing their understanding of themselves. Through articulating thoughts, ideas and perspectives it is possible to reflect on your own and others' thinking. The insights gained, if recognised, enable learning and a deeper understanding of our own and others' perspectives. As such it will inform our future conversations with colleagues and parents. In addition it will add to our thinking and interpretations of observations. For example, discussing why our interpretation makes sense, given what we already know about the child's thinking and understanding in other areas of learning. It is in the process of 'making the case' and providing evidence to support our view that a richer picture of our current understanding of the child is created. This is not just about arguing with other view points, but about exploring in more depth what has led to each possible interpretation of the observations. This sounds a long-winded and time consuming process. However, such conversations may be

short, often 5-10 minutes, so long as they are focused and adults are engaging supportively in the process for the benefit of the child.

Identifying the learning

After using both written and mental observations as a description of what is happening, a fully informed discussion can take place. Once the interpretations are considered, the next step is to identify the learning which is taking place. This gives a secure basis for identifying appropriate next steps. This process is common to all areas of learning. The regular reviewing of previous observations is important in looking for progress. It is also helpful in evidencing the effective strategies and approaches which are most supportive of a particular child's learning. This reflection on progress is particularly useful in thinking about children's social understanding and behaviour. For example, insights can be gained about the child's approaches to problem solving. Several responses are possible including:

- Giving up immediately

- Getting frustrated

- Asking the nearest adult to help

- Finding a specific adult to help

I think it was round here

The sequence of play tells a different story

- Asking another child to help

- Persevering with the same strategy even though it is not working

- Stopping and having a think

- Using strategies which have been effective previously

Understanding the ways children make connections with each other in a peer play situation can give a 'reality check' on their real life social confidences or uncertainties. Once engaged in play, it is useful to note how each individual child makes suggestions or directs the play. Again, these are specific skills and indicators of a child's confidence in interactions. By ensuring a balance of observations between peer play situations and times with adults, a realistic picture can be developed of the child's usual pattern of interactions. This will also enable consideration of differences between the two situations. Overall this approach provides evidence of the child's current ability to apply emerging social understanding.

Pretend play

A form of play which has received particular attention in the development of social understanding is the engagement in pretend play (Dunn 2004, Carpendale & Lewis, 2006). The importance of pretend play is that it requires participants to take part in an imaginary situation. The imaginary situation has to be independently understood so that players contribute to maintaining the game. The coherence of the game needs a common understanding of the pretend situation. Themes in research have focused on the ability of young children to engage in the complexities of such play. For example, being able to maintain the pretence that a box is a spaceship or that a playmate is 'being a Mummy' and to respond appropriately in the context of the shared understanding of the game. This process seems to need children to be able to 'hold' in mind a pretend world separate from a 'real' world and respond accordingly for the duration of the game. It also suggests that the participants are able to recognise that their playmates are also able to achieve this form of thinking. In essence, such complex play requires a shared understanding of meaning. Suggestions have been made from research that this is significant evidence of children's developing awareness of how their own and other's thinking works. Pretend play has also been highlighted as part of the process through which children can explore one another's perspective. Judy Dunn, for example, makes a clear distinction between pretend play, i.e., using a banana as a phone, and role play, i.e., taking the part of a character and responding as they think the character would in the situation. A further suggested important role for pretend play is to 'act out' experiences which may be exciting or worrying to a child. As they do this rehearsal type of activity, the suggestion is that they are able to think through and make sense of particular events.

The implication is that observations of engagement in pretend and role play could offer important insights into the child's developing social understanding. Firstly, the ability to share meaning through pretence seems important in recognising another's thinking and 'tuning in' to their thinking. Secondly, the way in which role play offers opportunities for exploring another's perspective on a situation may support real life understanding. Finally, being able to use pretend play as a means of making sense of situations and emotions may, for some children, be a useful tool in organising their thinking and feelings.

The various types of play in which a child takes part can be seen as an important expression of their current understanding of themselves and their relationships with others. Bringing together observations from different aspects of a child's play provides the opportunity for gaining deeper insight into the child's social understanding. As previously described, sharing interpretations of observations with colleagues is an important part of the process. The analysis of observations and collective knowledge about children's behaviour can take several forms. This can include:

- Frequent and regular review of an individual child's progress with colleagues and parents

- Focused observation of group interactions during play

- Time sampling observations i.e., a one minute observation every ten minutes for half an hour

- Shared observation – more than one adult (could include parents) observing the same activity, then comparing and discussing the key points noted and interpretation

- Noting frequency and context of a particular behaviour over a set period

- Antecedent, Behaviour, Consequence observation – the purpose of this is to identify what happened to trigger the behaviour and what happened as a consequence of the behaviour

- Sharing parent observations from home and practitioner observations from the setting.

It is helpful to remember that there are likely to be significant differences in these sources of information. Mainly this will be because children (like adults) will experience different intensities of emotions at home which will influence their reactions and behaviours.

Using 'can do' statements

A further useful tool in the analysis of observations is to construct a specific 'can do' statement related to the evidence in the observation. More detail about this approach is described in *Social Skills in the Early Years* (Mathieson, 2005). Briefly, it is a technique which helps to recognise the current successes which the child is experiencing. By reflecting on regular observations, it is possible to construct a statement which describes a specific behaviour. It seems to be most helpful if the 'can do' statement follows a specific format. This needs to include the:

- Observable behaviour

- Context

- Duration

The resultant statement would look something like the following examples:

- Aleisha can play alongside three other children in the construction area for three minutes.

- Jonathan can successfully join other boys' play on three out of four occasions during outdoor play.

This form of statement is useful because it provides direct evidence of the child's current ability. Once a clear statement of current achievement is constructed, the next step is to consider in what way it would be helpful to develop the learning. To ensure that expectations are realistic and relevant, the 'can do' statement is used as the basis. If only one of the three elements, observable behaviour, context or duration is changed, the next step will be clearly based on what the child 'can do' at this point in time. The next step can be described by changing one of the three elements i.e. playing alongside three other children, or in the construction area, or for three minutes. This would change the statement in the following way. For example, Aleisha will play alongside three other children in the construction area for five minutes. By making sure that only one element is changed, it is much more likely to ensure

Example: Purposeful use of observations

I can...if you give me time

Childminder

Angeline found sharing observations with parents was a particularly useful way of building parents' confidence and recognising progress in children's social understanding. She found that using observations of how Jamil and Peter approached other children to play sparked important discussions with their parents. The adults identified that the boys used different strategies at the park than when at the childminder's or their own home. By talking through and noting with parents the range of approaches the children used, they were able to see that when more confident they were more successful in joining others play. The adults agreed the next steps to support the children to feel confident. First, they talked with the children about different ways of asking to play. Secondly, they used puppets and Playmobile to explore the idea that others may not always want to play a particular game. Gradually, the children demonstrated more confidence in asking others to play and recognising that it was ok if they did not want to play on this occasion. Finally, Angeline made a photograph book of the children's learning journey which included the different ways they engaged others in play or said they did not want to play at this time. It also included examples of successful play at the park, home and at Angeline's house.

Pre-school

The staff at Jumble Tots Pre-school were concerned that they may not be thinking broadly enough about the interpretations of the children's behaviour. At the beginning of each planning or staff meeting they talked about an observation. They used an anonymous observation of a child playing in a group where they hit out at another child. From the basic observation the staff built a collection of as many different interpretations as possible. These included making contact, wanting the toy another child has, accidental contact while trying to get to another toy, wanting attention, anxiety that another child was too close, frustration that the toy had broken etc.

Day Nursery

The staff at Bembo's Day Nursery were worried about being fair and responding appropriately to a range of children's behaviour. They were keen to focus on the learning which would result for individual children. At a staff meeting they decided to use an observation scenario as the basis for discussion. As individuals

Example: Purposeful use of observations

Why might I be hiding?

and as a group they compared how they would interpret the scenario if different children were involved. For example, the first scenario involves children A, B and C – child A pushes child B, who screams and runs away. Child C then hits child A. First, the team talked about the various interpretations of the behaviour. Next they suggested how the adults might respond. Finally, they substituted different children for A, B and C. They had lots of useful discussion about whether the interpretation was the same each time. The most complex discussion was focused on whether the response would be different for each child and if so why might this be.

School

At Downe Primary School the reception class team was feeling frustrated that they did not have enough time to talk with each other about problems and concerns which emerged. During each room team planning meeting they decided to use five minutes for such discussions. At first this discussion quickly became very negative. The staff members who raised the concerns said they felt anxious that colleagues might judge their practice. All the team members agreed that the purpose of the discussion was

to devise strategies and think differently about individual children's social and behavioural learning. One member of the team suggested using a specific technique she had learned in a training course. Julie gave a brief outline of her concern. Each colleague then asked a question. Julie then wrote down the question which had been asked. It was very important that after the first description of the concern Julie did not say anything in response to the questions asked. This helped colleagues to develop their thinking about the concern without the distraction of discussion. Each question began to lead on from or add to the previous one. This helped to encourage deeper thinking and a broader range of ideas to be raised. The questions Julie had written down were then used as a prompt for her thinking, which she could share with colleagues as necessary.

Each subsequent meeting began with a comment about what had been useful to support the child's learning and the practitioner's reflection from the last meeting. The process was also reported by practitioners to have helped them generally to feel more confident about talking with colleagues and parents about behaviour.

expectations are realistic and are based on the child's current successes. A key point to remember when constructing such 'can do' statements is that the more detailed they are, the greater chance of success. Once the 'will' statement has been constructed and shared with the adults involved, the discussion needs to focus on the ways in which the adults can ensure the child has 'best possible chance' of success. This provides a good basis for reflection of the 'exceptions' in the child's patterns of responses. When are they most likely to be able to play alongside other children or join others' play? The observations and collective adult knowledge which contribute to this part of the process are crucial to its success. Where adults have noted the details such as times of day, which other children are involved, factors which may have helped the child feel more relaxed, etc., the more this knowledge can be used to support the child.

A frequent concern of both practitioners and parents is the length of time it takes to make changes to behaviour. Having gone through the process outlined above, there can be disappointment if there is not an immediate achievement of the next step. Realistically, changing behaviour is difficult and takes much longer. As a rough guide, consistently maintaining an agreed strategy will make a change to behaviour in a three week period. But the change noticed may not be the change hoped for, although it will add important information to the existing collective knowledge. As such it will inform and increase the chance of future success.

Actively seeking ways to develop staff confidence and curiosity about children's developing understanding of behaviour is an important aspect of professional development. There are several different ways of enhancing this learning such as:

- Reflecting with a colleague on a particular aspect of practice to assess its effectiveness

- Visiting a different setting nearby to share ideas and support each others learning

- Develop links with local children's centres, nursery schools and schools to support each other to keep up to date with changes in early years legislation, guidance, approaches and practice.

- Join a professional network or organisations such as Early Education, National Day Nursery Association, National Childminding Association, Pre-school Learning Alliance etc.

Building links with a range of colleagues helps to challenge and question existing practice and share new ideas. Fundamentally

LINKS WITH YOUR PRACTICE

A large part of the work we do in early years provision relies on observation skills and in depth knowledge and understanding of child development. Although most practitioners focus extensively on these topics in their initial training, it is essential to keep up to date and build on this basic foundation.

Training courses are a good starting point, but unless the new learning is put into practice it is likely to be rapidly lost. There are some useful things to consider about attending a training course:

- Is it the right course for you and the setting at this point in time? How do you know?

- Is the course being offered by a reputable, high quality organisation or trainer?

- What preparation and reflection on your current practice would be helpful before you attend?

- Are there some specific things you would like to find out on the course?

- What pre-reading around the course topic might be useful to increase your understanding and learning?

- In what way will you be able to feed back to other members of your staff team?

- In what ways will the leadership team support you to implement agreed changes to practice?

- After the course in what other ways might your learning and understanding be extended?

Attending training courses is not the only way to improve current practice, knowledge and understanding. You may also want to think about:

- Having a topic for staff discussion with everyone contributing to and sharing the learning

- Talking to key members of the staff team about different aspects of children's development or learning

it helps to keep interest alive as well as enhancing enthusiasm for understanding children's learning. One element of this is to develop confidence in using different forms of observation and being able to talk through with other practitioners the advantages and disadvantages of each. This can lead on to sharing ideas about the organisation of notes and recording of observations. As previously mentioned as adults we are observing all the time but recognising what is significant and useful to record in a particular way is also important. Further, making sure that observations are put to good use and organised in a way which is helpful ensures that they are benefitting the children's learning.

The focused observation of children's play is particularly useful to gain insights into their real life social understanding. An overview of observations is important to give a realistic picture of children's skills and abilities so consideration of the following will be helpful:

- Do observations reflect a balance of play opportunities i.e., inside, outside, independently, with friends, with a small/large peer group, with a range of equipment etc.?

- Are there trends in children's current play i.e., do boys/girls tend to play together/outside/large groups/small groups, do older/younger children tend to have particular patterns of play?

- In what ways are children making contact with each other?

- In what ways are children 'asking' to join a particular game?

- What is the first response from children when there is a conflict ?

- Which children seek out others to play with ?

- Which children are sought out by others to play?

- Which children generally prefer very active play?

- Which children generally prefer less active play?

- Which children generally prefer loud play situations?

- Which children generally prefer quiet play situations?

Building detailed knowledge of children's usual patterns of play can be helpful to add insights into the situations in which they feel most at ease and confident in their interactions with others. This can help adults to reflect on the learning environment and ways in which they can build on children's existing confidences and abilities.

Having observed the children's social connections in this way the next step is to reflect on how routines and adult responses support and model appropriate interactions. For example, there are several opportunities during the day when adults will invite children to take part in activities. This can easily be used to model appropriate language and behavioural responses. Engaging several children in the process can enable important rehearsal opportunities which can build individual children's confidence.

Special Educational Needs

There are, of course, some children for whom their social, emotional and behavioural learning is influenced by an additional or special educational need. This can take a variety of forms but there are some general points which it is helpful to bear in mind. Any child with additional needs is firstly a child in their own right and will benefit from positive interactions with other children as well as adults. Other children too will benefit from positive interactions with children with additional needs. It is a key message for early years settings to communicate that they welcome the diversity of the local population and are proactive in their inclusive approaches to engaging all children and families.

In some cases a child's needs will already have been identified. Those first impressions when a family come to visit are crucial. As they decide if they will take up a place the reactions of the adults will set the tone for the future relationship. The same quality of welcome and interest needs to be afforded to all families. However, a first meeting where a child has identified additional needs can raise particular emotions for both the parents and practitioners. There may be increased anxiety and sensitivity about whether the special needs will be given greater importance than the child's strengths, abilities and future progress. Practitioners, on the other hand may be anxious to say 'the right thing' worried the child's needs may be very difficult to deal with and mean extra and unfamiliar paperwork or support. At this first meeting the parent is obviously more aware of the child's needs and the likely difficulties which may follow. The practitioner's openness and desire to bridge the gap is essential at this stage. Such an approach can at least begin to build a positive and open relationship. A useful starting point may be to think about things from the child's perspective. Exploring with the parent the child's everyday experiences can really help to reduce anxiety and tension. By talking through normal daily routines at home parents have a very practical opportunity to share their

We want to play together!

Sometimes I want to play on my own!

problem solving strategies. Developing such a conversation to think about similarities with the setting routines can help to pre-empt many issues. In most cases potential concerns or barriers can be explored and resolved.

Where practitioners and settings have little or no experience in working with children with additional needs it is important to seek out appropriate advice and support. There are many sources for valuable help, firstly, parents can provide extensive insights into ways to include their child. Secondly, making connections with other settings who have effectively included children with a range of needs can be a helpful partnership.

Ideally, practitioners will be aware of, and have regular contact with local authority Early Years SEN and inclusion support teams. On-going training if not directly delivered by local authority teams can be recommended by them. This is particularly relevant for the SENCO/Inclusion Coordinator who needs to regularly update their training. Another very useful link to establish and nurture is with the local health visiting, social care team and health centre. The local Family Information Service and nearest children's centre is a good starting point to begin building such support networks. Knowing about and keeping in touch with these sources of support and guidance should make preparing for and welcoming a child with additional needs much smoother and less stressful for all concerned.

Whichever agencies and professionals are involved with the family and child there will be regular reviews of the child's developmental progress. Given that the child is likely to spend considerable time in the setting it is important that this is reflected in these reviews. As a part of monitoring achievements, progress and development the settings observations and evidence will be a significant contribution to the child's records. They are also likely to be used for multi-agency reviews and should be available for parents to take to annual reviews or progress meetings with key professionals involved with the child. Examples of effective practice such as through the Early Support materials highlight the benefit of sharing any reports and information before submitting to such reviews.

In reality, early years settings are often also in the position of raising concerns about children's developmental progress that may later be recognised as early identification of a special educational need. In this situation too observation and analysis showing rate of progress, particular strengths, effective strategies and detailed next steps. Specifically working with parents to compile a clear picture of strengths and effective support helps to gradually work out the most appropriate way to help the child to progress. Many of the points raised earlier in this chapter are obviously also important in this situation. The partnership relationship with parents is central to being able to offer and find the right kind of support as things

In how many ways do I make connections?

Sharing what we think we see

progress. The core principles of trust, respect and advocacy will underpin the most effective professional relationships with children and their families.

Through attendance at local training, SENCOs and managers in particular, will be able to keep up to date with local protocols. This will include use of and contributions to Common Assessment Framework procedures, allocation of Lead Professionals and Safeguarding procedures. Not all settings will have children with special needs all of the time and local protocols are regularly reviewed and improved. It is

essential to be proactive in checking that setting policy and practice is in line with relevant and current guidance.

Using Internet based sources of information can be useful but always check the credibility of the website. The most relevant for your situation are likely to be UK based, national organizations such as the department of health/education, local authority websites, charity and voluntary sector support groups. For medical conditions the Great Ormond Street Hospital has a web based resources for parents which gives an outline of specific conditions and their implications.

KEY POINTS IN THINKING ABOUT BEHAVIOUR AS AN AREA OF LEARNING

- The interpretation of observations is more likely to be helpful to children's learning if they are discussed with colleagues and parents

- Observations of children's peer play, including pretend or role play can provide valuable insights into their current social understanding

- Reviewing observations to clarify progress and 'can do' statements provides a strong evidence base for building

effective strategies. Changing one element of the statement ensures realistic expectations of progress

- For families with children with additional needs establishing a positive partnership relationship right from the start is even more important

- Attending training and sharing new learning is essential to keeping our thinking fresh and questioning our own practice

References

Buss K A, Kiel E J (2004) Comparison of sadness, anger, and fear facial expressions when toddlers look at their mothers. *Child Development*, 75(6), 1761-1773.

Denham S (1986) Social cognition, prosocial behaviour and emotion in preschoolers: Contextual validation. *Child Development*, 57(1), 194-201.

Denham S, Mason T, Caverly S, Schmidt M, Hackney R, Caswell C, et al. (2001) Preschoolers at Play:Co-socialisers of emotional and social competence. *International Journal of Behavioral Development*, 25(4), 290-301.

Dowling M (2005) *Young Children's Personal, Social and Emotional Development*. Second Edition. Paul Chapman Publishing, London, UK.

Dunn J (2004) *Children's Friendships: The Beginnings of Intimacy*. Blackwell Publishing Ltd, Oxford UK.

Fabes R A, Eisenberg N, Hanish L D, Spinrad T L (2001) Preschoolers spontaneous emotion vocabulary: Relations to likeability. *Early Education and Development*, 12(1), 11-27.

Greenfield S (2000) *Brain Story*. BBC Worldwide Ltd, London, UK.

Greenfield S (2000) T*he Private Life of the Brain*. Penguin, London, UK.

Halberstadt A G, Denham S, Dunsmore J C (2001) Affective Social Competence. *Social Development*, 10(1), 79-119.

Keenan T (2002) *An Introduction to Child Development*. Sage Publications Ltd, London UK.

Krueger F, Barbey A K, Grafman J (2009) The medial prefrontal cortex mediates social event knowledge. *Trends in Cognitive Sciences*, 13(3), 103-109.

Lindon J (2008/9) *What does it mean to be...?* Practical Pre-School Books, London, UK.

Lindon J (2009) *Parents as Partners: Positive Relationships in the Early Years*. Practical Pre-School Books, London, UK.

Mathieson K, Banerjee R (2010) Pre-school peer play: The beginnings of social competence. *Educational and Child Psychology*, 27(1), 9-20.

Roberts K (2009) *Early Home Learning Matters. A good practice guide*. Family and Parenting Institute, London, UK.

Rogers B, McPherson E (2008) Behaviour Management with Young Children. Sage, London, UK.

Schaffer H R (1996) *Social Development*. Blackwell Publishing Ltd, Oxford, UK.

Schore A (1994) *Affect Regulation and the Origin of the Self, hillside*. Lawrence Erlbaum Associates Inc., New Jersey, USA.

Sylva K, Melhuish E, Sammons P, Siraj-Blatchford I, Taggart B (2010) *Early Childhood Matters: Evidence from the effective pre-school and primary education project*. Routledge, Oxon, UK.

Trevarthen C, Aitken K J (2001) Infant intersubjectivity: Research, theory, and clinical applications. *Journal of Child Psychology and Psychiatry*, vol 42, 1 pp3-48.

Ward J (2012) *The Student's Guide to Social Neuroscience*. Psychology Press, East Sussex, UK.

Wellman H M, Cross D, Watson J (2001) Meta-analysis of theory of mind development: The truth about false belief. *Child Development*, 72(3), 655-684.

Additional sources of information

Publications

Athey C (2007) *Extending Thought in Young Children. A parent-teacher partnership*. Paul Chapman Publishing, London, UK.

Brownell C A, Kopp C (2007) *Socioemotional Development in the Toddler Years*. The Guilford Press, New York, USA.

DCSF (2010) *Inclusion Development Programme Supporting Children with Behavioural, Emotional and Social Difficulties: Guidance for practitioners in the Early Years Foundation Stage*. The National Strategies DCSF Publication (available from www.gov.uk/publications).

DCSF (2008) *Social and Emotional Aspects of Development*. The National Strategies DCSF Publication (available from http://webarchive.nationalarchives.gov.uk).

Dorman H, Dorman C (2002) *The Social Toddler*. CP Publishing, Richmond, Surrey, UK.

Dunn J (1993) *Young Children's Close Relationships*. Sage Publications Ltd, London UK.

Fernyhough C (2008) *The Baby in the Mirror*. Granta Publications, London, UK.

Gopnik A (2009) *The Philosophical Baby*. The Bodely Head, London, UK.

Hobson P (2002) *The Cradle of Thought, exploring the origins of thinking*. Pan Macmillan, London, UK.

Mathieson K (2005) *Social Skills in the Early Years*. Paul Chapman Publishing, London, UK.

Mathieson K (2007) *Identifying Special Needs in the Early Years*. Paul Chapman Publishing, London, UK.

Murray L, Andrews L (2005) *The Social Baby*. CP Publishing, Richmond, Surrey, UK.

Nutbrown C, Clough P, Selbie P (2008) *Early Childhood Education*. Sage Publications Ltd, London UK.

Parkinson B, Fischer A H, Manstead A S R (2005) *Emotions in Social Relations*. Psychology Press, New York, USA.

Robinson M (2003) *From Birth to One The year of opportunity*. Open University Press, Buckingham, UK.

Sylva K, Melhuish E, Sammons P, Siraj-Blatchford I, Taggart B (eds) (2010) *Early Childhood Matters Evidence from the Effective Pre-School and Primary Education project*. Routledge, London, UK.

Websites

www.education.gov.uk

www.nhs.uk

www.early-education.org.uk

www.gosh.nhs.uk

www.ntpi.org.uk (National Family and Parenting Institute)

www.parentlineplus.org.uk

Finding help and support

The quality of early years provision in the UK at this time can vary considerably from setting to setting. There are a range of indicators which give information about the current quality of a setting. These include:

- Local authority information and notes of visits from Early Years support teams

- Leadership and management understanding of the importance of individual children's progress and development and ability to effectively work in partnership with parents

- Staff qualifications

- Training attended

- The evidence of impact of training

- Use of supervision as well as performance management/appraisal systems

- Effective implementation of the Early Years Foundation Stage

- Ofsted comments and judgements

- The setting Self-Evaluation Form

In your setting

As an individual practitioner you can make important decisions about your own practice and how to improve it. This is likely to include thinking about some of the bullet points above. But it will also involve working with colleagues to create a positive and supportive emotional environment which encourages everyone's learning – adults and children. We each have the responsibility to take on simple actions and ways of interacting which encourage and support rather than 'put down' or ridicule our own or others' achievements. Each thing we say and do contributes to the emotional environment in which we work and our children grow.

Each individual also impacts on the approach of the room team, atmosphere of staff meetings and the opportunity for good leadership to thrive. Working as a team to improve the quality of the setting and the relationships in it makes our working day more enjoyable and effective.

Finding other colleagues who, like you, wish to build such a positive way of working increases the impact you can have. Sharing ideas, understanding and knowledge is a great way to begin.

Local community

In your local community there will be a variety of sources of support and information. The local library as well as being an important source for reference and details of new research will have other information which can support you. Childcare is an important part of the local community whether provided by maintained, private voluntary or independent providers. The library will have information about different activities, training courses, voluntary sector groups which work with children and families. Exploring what is available in your local area can extend your experience as well as highlight other possible sources of support for families and colleagues.

Local authority

At the present time many local authorities are changing the way in which they offer support and training to the childcare practitioners in their area. Your authority may still be providing training and quality improvement services or they may be buying this in from independent sources when needed. Your local authority website or offices will be able to give you current information.

Acknowledgements

This book has only been possible because of the many children, families and practitioners with whom I have worked over many years. I am constantly impressed by the dedication, care and hard work which practitioners demonstrate in their work with our young children. It is a most challenging job and on some days it can feel overwhelming, in similar ways to being a parent. Over recent years I have seen a significant increase in the professionalism of practitioners and their drive to improve the quality of provision for children is impressive.

In particular, I would like to thank two early years settings who have made major contributions to this book. Firstly, Becca Robinson, the staff and parents at Whytebeams Nursery School and secondly Caroline King, the staff and parents at Pegasus Academy Children's Centre for their continued support and for allowing me to use the fantastic photographs.